Experiencing God's Power in Your Ministry

Mary Southerland

HARVEST HOUSE PUBLISHERS

EUGENE, OREGON

Cover by Garborg Design Works, Minneapolis, Minnesota

Cover photo © Steven Plummer/Garborg Design Works

EXPERIENCING GOD'S POWER IN YOUR MINISTRY
Copyright © 2006 by Mary Southerland
Published by Harvest House Publishers
Eugene, Oregon 97402
www.harvesthousepublishers.com

Library of Congress Cataloging-in-Publication Data
Southerland, Mary.
  Experiencing God's power in your ministry / Mary Southerland.
    p. cm.
  ISBN-13: 978-0-7369-1612-7 (pbk.)
  ISBN-10: 0-7369-1612-1
  1. Women in church work.   2. Church work.   I. Title.
  BV4415.S67 2006
  253'.082—dc22   2005023333

Printed in the United States of America

06 07 08 09 10 11 12 13 14 /VP-CF/ 10 9 8 7 6 5 4 3 2 1

Experiencing God's Power in Your Ministry is
dedicated to every woman who serves God. You are
amazing! The fact is…each one of you is my hero!

Your commitment to God challenges me as a woman in
ministry to serve Him with greater passion and higher purpose.
Your faith spurs me on to see the invisible, believe the incredible,
and dream the impossible. Your strength causes me to hope.
When I am tempted to give up and give in, I remember you
and celebrate the reassuring truth that I am not alone. We
battle the darkness together, and God is with us! We run the
same race…teammates…not in competition, but as one.

Thank you for your faithfulness when it seems that no one
knows. God does. Thank you for your willingness to embrace
those shunned by others. God sees. Thank you for standing
firm when you feel like giving up. God understands.

I pray that the journey ahead may be filled with joy. I long for
the day when, together, we stand before the Father, our lives a sweet-
smelling sacrifice and an acceptable offering of praise to Him, the One
who shaped us for service. My friend, please accept this book as a gift
from one who celebrates your life and calling as a woman in ministry.

Contents

❦ ❦ ❦

Our only power and success come from God.

2 CORINTHIANS 3:5

❦ ❦ ❦

As You Begin...

The book you hold in your hand was written with a "tell it like it is" mentality. I have prayed that God would wrap each word in transparency, birth it out of integrity, and empower it in our lives. This book is not just for the woman on a church staff or the wife of a pastor—if you are a woman serving God in any way, you are a woman in ministry, and this book was written for you.

I have often scoured bookstore shelves in search of resources for women in ministry, only to be disappointed. My husband, Dan, silenced my complaints with, "Honey, if you can't find a book for women in ministry, maybe God wants you to write it."

And I knew *Experiencing God's Power in Your Ministry* was a "God-thing" the minute I handed the proposal to Barb Sherrill, a precious friend and an editor with Harvest House Publishers. "I don't believe this!" she said. "In a meeting last week, we talked about asking you to write a book for women in ministry. And here it is!" I love it when a plan comes together!

About the Chapters

A ministry without purpose is powerless. The same is true for us personally. Each chapter in *Experiencing God's Power in Your Ministry* is based on a principle of purpose:

P   Perceive your worth
U   Unleash your faith
R   Relish Godly discipline
P   Pursue God's vision
O   Opt for peace
S   Strive for greatness
E   Endure the storms

To experience the life-changing power of God in ministry, we must serve *from* God's purpose—instead of plunging into ministry, hoping that God's purpose will surface somewhere along the way.

About the Study Sections

Each chapter includes a section called "Studying It Out." Don't skip these Bible studies! Take time to sit at His feet, basking in His truth, simply because He is your God and you are His child—not because you have a sermon to prepare or a Bible study to facilitate. The Word of God is the only solid ground in life and is our power source for ministry.

About the Life Stories

I have had the privilege of meeting and working with some incredible women in ministry! The longer I serve Him, the more I realize just how much we need each other. Look for your own journey in the lives of these women. Learn from them, be challenged by their journeys, and cheer them on. To celebrate God at work in the lives of other women in ministry is to celebrate God Himself.

This One's for You!

know I may be dating myself a bit when I say I absolutely *love* the music of Barry Manilow. His simple but penetrating lyrics and haunting melodies linger gently in my heart and mind long after the song has ended. As I began writing this book, words from a favorite Manilow tune, "This One's for You," skipped through my thoughts. Those words aptly explain the very reason this book exists: for you—wherever you might be, as the song goes on to say—a woman in ministry.

Being in ministry is still an amazing gift I unwrap each day. There is no greater joy than to be used by God. To see Him change lives while allowing me to be a small part of the process is still an astonishing reality in my life. Almost daily, I think back over the years of serving Him in churches, at youth camps, on mission trips, and now, in a speaking and writing ministry—not to mention the spectacularly ordinary details of everyday living. Like you, I revel in His calling on my life as a woman in ministry.

I also know that, at times, your days are painfully long, your nights dark and lonely. Schedule demands repeatedly overwhelm you, draining the once treasured joy of service from your heart and soul. It seems everyone needs your time and energy, clamors for your attention, and demands your presence. Solitude is swallowed up by the agendas and expectations of others. Activities fill your calendar, drawing you away from the most important thing—the unseen power of sitting at the feet of Jesus, soaking in His truth, and being restored by His presence. People occasionally misunderstand you and hold you to an unholy standard, while your own heart wrestles with condemning insecurity and paralyzing doubt.

Just when you are ready to give up, a friend writes an encouraging note, thanking you for making a difference in her life. Church members unexpectedly deliver a scrumptious hot meal to your front door "just because they love you," saving you and your family from another paper-wrapped food experience. An elderly couple offers to take your children to dinner and a movie so you and your husband can enjoy a quiet evening at home—alone. The thrill of seeing lives redeemed and destinies altered is beyond compare.

You may be faithfully serving God in a small country church where planting and harvesting times determine the size of your congregation. A poverty-stricken ghetto or an exclusive country-club community may be your mission field. Your church may sit in the middle of a foreign land or in the familiar neighborhood where you were raised. You may encourage and support your husband as he pastors, or you may be a pastor. Your heart passion may be leading a Bible study for the women in your neighborhood, visiting the sick, or teaching a children's Sunday-school class. While our circumstances are vastly different, our needs are much the same—as are the habits that make us effective in ministry.

There are times I feel as if I have been in ministry forever. More often than not, I say those words with absolute joy and a thankful, wonder-filled heart that cannot understand why God would ever choose me for anything remotely related to kingdom work. To be honest, there are also times when I desperately want to turn and walk away, leaving ministry to tougher-skinned servants. Invariably, it is in those uncertain moments that His persistent love gently draws me back to the only place I have ever found peace and purpose—the center of His will for my life—being a woman in ministry.

I started at a young age, as the director of a ten-member children's choir—the "Junior Choir," as it was called. I was soon singing solos and playing the piano for worship services in the small country church I attended. In high school I became a summer missionary. After college I served on several church staffs as a youth and music assistant then moved into teaching women and—well, here I am today, a former youth director, a pastor's wife, the mother of two, the director of women's ministries, a conference speaker, Bible study teacher and author, all of which has made the previous 37 years of my life an incredible and anything-but-boring journey!

The dark times and staggering seasons of pain have yielded those precious "treasures of darkness, and riches stored in secret places" the prophet Isaiah describes in Isaiah 45:3 (NIV). Mountaintop experiences have left me immersed in God's stubborn love, His unfailing power, and His perpetual faithfulness to this too-often-faithless child. I am finally coming to the place in ministry where I can truly "count it all joy," knowing that God is enough—no, He's more than enough—for every need, every breath, every trial, and every step of the way through this life passage we call ministry.

Success That Endures

We all want to be successful in ministry. The problem is, we often mistakenly settle for a temporary and superficial success instead of the eternal and unfathomable success God offers, buying into the false truths and skewed perspectives of religious power brokers. Sadly enough, success in ministry is often defined by the size of the church we serve, the title and position we hold, or the power and prestige we possess in the religious arena! The apostle Paul impressively nails these base thoughts when he writes,

> It is not that we think we can do anything of lasting value by ourselves. Our only power and success come from God (2 Corinthians 3:5).

God does not condemn power and success—unless it is the defective human power or the shallow success that we manage to produce in our strength alone. Human success feeds human appetites such as pride, greed, lust, vanity. Instead, God offers His divine, unshakable power backed by the honor of His character and the authority of His name. His power alone can achieve the uncorrupted, genuine success that endures.

> God offers His divine, unshakable power backed by the honor of His character and the authority of His name. His power alone can achieve the uncorrupted, genuine success that endures.

For the power of God to reign in our lives and flow through us in effective, purpose-driven ministry, we must nurture certain spiritual habits. Habits can be good or bad, but they are all powerful motivators—learned patterns and spiritual choices that ultimately determine the difference between failure and success in life as well as ministry. The good news about habits is, while they are spiritual disciplines, ours to establish and ours to control, they are God's alone to empower.

Too many women allow immediate needs and urgent demands to determine the path their ministry will take and set the life course they will run, instead of relying on God's direction spelled out through godly habits. God's plan and calling is always certain, flowing from a meticulous step-by-step strategy that fulfills His purpose in us and accomplishes His kingdom work through us. Ours is a holy calling, a divine life mission—that all of hell will surely stand against. The battle is so fierce because the stakes are so high. Eternity hangs in the balance for those God gives to us in ministry.

It is my burning prayer that this book will encourage you as a woman in ministry to celebrate God's call on your life, abandon yourself to His plan, and embrace His purpose in a fresh, desperate obedience. I invite you to join me in cultivating those spiritual habits that honor God and compel us to become fully devoted followers of Jesus Christ. May this book lead us all to discover our highest purpose and most powerful place of service in and through Jesus Christ, the One who created us, gifted us, and called us to His side as women in ministry.

The Key to Powerful Ministry
A Life Story by Rachel Olsen

Rachel Olsen *is a dynamic teacher who speaks with wisdom women need, humor they enjoy, and sincerity they remember. Rachel is available for women's events through Proverbs 31 Ministries at 1-877-731-4663. She and her husband, Rick Olsen, PhD, are available for couple's events through www .christianspeakers4you.com.*

It's not rocket science, but it took me a while to realize that a fundamental key to ministering in God's power is recognizing where my efforts end and His plans begin. Let me explain why I have often missed this simple but essential truth.

Like each of His children, I'm blessed with certain God-given gifts and talents which help me excel in life and ministry. For instance, I'm a creative thinker. A capacity for brainstorming and problem-solving seems to be hard-wired into my DNA. For that reason, I'm often looked to for input or guidance. I'm also a good communicator, so I'm generally able to persuade others to my point of view, or to take my proposed course of action. Therefore, I am frequently pegged for leadership positions. While these assets are God-given, it is my responsibility to hone and develop them through education, use, and training. Above all, I have to be careful to lead others to experience *God's* best—and not simply the best I can come up with.

I can easily do my own (albeit noble) thing and do it well enough that the general assumption is, "This is God," when in reality, this is just Rachel operating in her own strength. Occasionally, the results are disastrous, most of the time they turn out good but not stellar, and once in a while they turn out great—only by the grace of God. The point is, as good as the Rachel-thing can sometimes be, the women I serve need a *God-thing* instead of my dog-and-pony show.

When I do get sidetracked into my own strength, I know God can bring good out of it as He redirects me back into alignment with His will. However, I may have missed some of the opportunities God ordained for me, and I may have cheated others out of their opportunities as well. A lot of people can be affected when we do our own thing and ask God to bless it, rather than waiting on His plans to be revealed.

Several years ago, I was asked to lead a church's ministry to mothers. I had served on their leadership team for a couple of years but did not feel a peace about taking the helm. The woman who did assume the leadership was asked to resign after six months. Another woman stepped into the position, but within six months she decided to leave the ministry altogether.

At that point, I wondered if I had missed God. Was I supposed to be leading this group? Without hesitation, I said yes when they again asked me to direct the group. I immediately sensed that I—if not the whole ministry—was operating outside of God's plan and will. What had once come so easily to me became a fruitless struggle! I repeatedly tried to talk to the church's leadership about it, to little avail. After four difficult months, I offered my resignation—a difficult decision because I felt like I was quitting midstream and letting people down. It was rather easy for them, therefore, to talk me out of resigning. I stayed on for two miserable months before resigning. My team suffered. I suffered. My family suffered. After resigning for good, I experienced spiritual renewal—and the ministry operated for one more year before closing down.

This experience convinced me I never again want to be involved in any ministry that is not ordained for me by God—even if it's a noble cause, even if it's well-attended, or even if I'm a "natural" for the job. For me, learning how God has gifted me was step one. The second step was learning when, where, and how to use those gifts under His guidance.

I now willingly sacrifice my talents and plans on His altar. Taking my cue from Jesus, I pray over the things I am most passionate about keeping, accomplishing, or attaining, "Not my will but Yours be done." Honestly, I sometimes have to pray those words repeatedly until I can mean them! In Deuteronomy 5:30-33, God said to His chosen leader Moses,

> Go and tell them to return to their tents. But you stay here with me so I can give you all my commands, laws, and regulations. You will teach them to the people so they can obey them in the land I am giving to them as their inheritance.

Like Moses, before I can teach or lead others, I must first be attuned to God's will. Like the people Moses instructed, I have to stay on track with God as I earnestly pray for Him to keep me—with all my grand ideas—in the center of His will.

I also purpose not to say yes to anything without thoughtful prayer and consideration—no matter how great the need or who asks me to do it. It is easy to assume that our leaders or mentors are so plugged into God that they always know what we should be doing. Sometimes they do, but sometimes they don't. I also run everything by my husband for his input, perspective, and approval before committing myself to a task.

No matter how wholesome the intention or how fine the execution, anything I do is but filthy rags compared to accomplishing what God has planned for me. That reality is sometimes hard to remember when an influential person calls with a great opportunity for you…or when your team's brainstorming session produces a novel idea you're sure will be a hit…or when God seems to have forgotten about your dreams and you feel the need to "get things rolling." I've found His plans to be perfect and His timing impeccable.

Like I said, it's not rocket science, but choosing to stay within God's will and strength rather than our own is a powerful principle that can launch our ministry into new levels of power.

🐜 🐜 🐜

Perceive Your Worth

Women in ministry often labor under the misconception they have to be an accomplished singer, wonderful keyboardist, or seminary-trained Bible teacher in order to qualify as the consummate minister's wife. I know women who really believe they have to be Betty Crocker to be godly. Not true!

As a high-school junior, I decided it was time to take Homemaking 101. I can still see Mrs. Johnson's face as she naïvely gazed at her new students. Bless her unsuspecting heart! She had no idea of the challenge I brought to that class and her career as a teacher. For weeks, I muddled through each lesson with a respectable but less-than-stellar performance—until we hit the section on sewing. It would prove to be her undoing where I was concerned.

Being the veteran teacher she was, Mrs. Johnson took a deep breath and doggedly plunged ahead in determination, vowing she could teach anyone to sew—even me. I decided to make a blouse, and I chose what I thought was a simple McCall's pattern. Mrs. Johnson was thrilled with my selection, confident that even I could make a blouse requiring approximately seven straight seams. The pattern looked so simple and even pretty in the package. Then I opened it, gingerly unfolding and carefully arranging each delicate pattern piece, staring at the foreign documents before me. They were simply beyond human comprehension. I concluded the pattern was actually a sinister trap designed by some accomplished but sadistic seamstress, and I quickly stuffed the flimsy elements back into their package. After all, I was creative! I didn't need a pattern! I knew exactly what I wanted to make, and how hard could it be? (Ignorance really can be bliss!)

When I presented the completed blouse to Mrs. Johnson for a grade, her eyes widened as she stared in silence at my first and last attempt at sewing. "Interesting," she muttered, obviously in shock. I made a "C" in her class, a sympathy grade if there ever was one. And the blouse? I buried it in my back yard—literally. Since that day, I always make sure I have at least one friend who can sew, as well as the names of two seamstresses on hand at all times. However, in all my years of ministry, I can truthfully say my inability to sew has never hindered God's work in my life or my calling as a woman in ministry.

Some have even dared to suggest that since I have a daughter, I should not only sew, but teach her to sew. (I buried that proposal along with Mrs. Johnson's blouse.) Another line of thinking has proposed that because I am a pastor's wife, I should drag out my silver (if I had any) and host dinners and teas for the women of the church. (Please know that those of you who actually enjoy these torturous events have my undying admiration and respect.) In our first full-time church, I actually gave it a shot by inviting the entire church to our home for a Christmas open house. Since there were several hundred church members at the time, I concluded it would take three nights to accommodate them all. Looking back, my only defense is a complete loss of sanity.

My family aptly dubbed the month before the first open house as "The Month from Hell." They had good reason. I put them all to work, cleaning and scrubbing every square inch of the house. I bought and hoarded food, threatening to hurt anyone who even thought about invading my "stash." I even managed to destroy Thanksgiving weekend by insisting that we decorate, inside and out, for Christmas—not in anticipation of celebrating Christ's birth, but in preparation for the "open houses" to be held the following weekend.

For three years, I tried to be the "hostess with the mostest," until my husband put a stop to the madness by asking one simple question: "Honey, why are you doing these open houses? You obviously don't enjoy them." The answer that popped into my mind and out of my mouth was absurd. "Because that's what pastor's wives do!" I feebly responded. "Where does it say that, honey?" he asked. Dan went on to set me free. "We have done our last open house. Please don't ever do anything else as a woman in ministry because you think it fits the man-made profile of a pastor's wife. Do what God has gifted and called you to do—period—and never apologize to anyone for doing so." I do not have the gift of hospitality, but in every church we have ever served, there have been women who do and who delight in using that gift for Him.

Who Is Your Audience?

It was Thursday morning, and time for my weekly appointment at our neighborhood deli. Carol, the deli manager, met me at the door with a warm smile and silently led the way to my "usual" booth, signaling the waitress to bring my "usual" order of a toasted bagel, fruit cup, and Diet Coke. I know—not the breakfast of champions, but it worked for me. "Who is it this week?" Carol asked as she cleaned and set the table. "Today I'm meeting a young pastor's wife who is ready to bolt!" I responded. "In that case," she grinned, "I'll bring lots of coffee and Kleenex." As Carol turned to leave, a beautiful but obviously frazzled young woman burst through the main door, hurriedly scanned the crowded deli, and made a beeline for me as if the ship was sinking and I was the last lifeboat. "Good luck!" Carol murmured, escaping into the kitchen.

I took a deep breath and prayed for wisdom as Kerry stumbled into the booth, heaving a huge sigh of relief. "I made it!" she gasped. With my most encouraging smile, I leaned across the table, squeezed her hand, and said, "Relax, Kerry. Take a deep breath. Everything is going to be all right." When her eyes met mine, she promptly burst into tears. (I have that effect on a lot of people, but it usually takes a little longer to kick in.) After gaining a measure of control, this young pastor's wife shared a wounded heart filled with pain and frustration.

Fresh out of seminary, Kerry's husband was the pastor of a small and struggling local church with the well-deserved reputation of eating pastors alive. It was their first full-time church and, as far as I could tell, a disaster in the making for all concerned. Her next words confirmed my evaluation. "Last night, the deacons handed my husband a list of 27 changes they feel I need to make in order to be the right kind of pastor's wife. Everything from the way I dress to where I sit during the service." I thought I had heard it all. After all, Dan and I had been in ministry for more than 20 years and had counseled hundreds of pastors and their wives, but I had to admit that a printed list of requirements for the pastor's wife was not only a new idea to me but, in my opinion, was straight from the pit and smelled like smoke.

Then it hit me. "Kerry, did you say the deacons handed this list to your *husband?*" "Yes," she wailed. "He's trying to keep the deacons happy, so he brought the list home and asked me to consider their requests." It was probably a blessing that my calendar was crammed full and finances were tight because I had neither time for jail nor money for bail—both of which I would need after being arrested for clobbering Kerry's husband! "Mary, I don't think I can do this. Maybe I'm not good enough to be a pastor's wife. I'm not a Bible scholar. I've been a Christian for only five years, and I can't even sing or play the piano. I don't like sitting on the front row, and I really prefer wearing pantsuits instead of dresses." I had heard enough.

Leaning across the table, I asked the same question that had changed my life and ministry years before, "Kerry, who is your audience?" Confused, she responded, "I don't know what you mean." "Exactly," I shot back. "Kerry, even Jesus couldn't please everyone, so why do you think you can? Who is your audience?"

Breakfast turned into lunch as I shared my own struggle with insecurity and fear as a woman in ministry, celebrating the truth that God delights in using the unlikely servant, the ordinary woman to accomplish extraordinary kingdom work. A tiny seed of hope was planted in Kerry's heart that morning as we searched Scripture, praying we would both learn to see ourselves through the eyes of God. Over the next few years, I watched her grow into a confident and capable pastor's wife who found her worth in God and ran the race for an audience of One.

A powerful woman in ministry has been set free from the prison of unrealistic expectations and damaged beliefs. A powerful woman in ministry understands the pivotal truth that her worth rests in God alone and that He is always in search of an empty, broken vessel, waiting to be filled with His authority. Our value rests in Him. Yet so many women in ministry never get to this truth. Instead, we are caught up in the religious trappings of comparison and competition. No matter what we do or how we do it, it is never quite good enough.

The Bible is filled with men and women who were unlikely servants. Weak, fearful, and unwilling, they fought against the call of God, offering excuses and pleading for exemption—just like we do as women in ministry. Gideon was such a man.

> The angel of the Lord came and sat down under the oak
> in Ophrah that belonged to Joash the Abiezrite, where

his son Gideon was threshing wheat in a winepress to keep it from the Midianites. When the angel of the LORD appeared to Gideon, he said, "The LORD is with you, mighty warrior." "But sir," Gideon replied, "if the LORD is with us, why has all this happened to us? Where are all his wonders that our fathers told us about when they said, 'Did not the LORD bring us up out of Egypt?' But now the LORD has abandoned us and put us into the hand of Midian." The LORD turned to him and said, "Go in the strength you have and save Israel out of Midian's hand. Am I not sending you?" "But LORD," Gideon asked, "how can I save Israel? My clan is the weakest in Manasseh, and I am the least in my family." The LORD answered, "I will be with you, and you will strike down all the Midianites together" (Judges 6:11-16 NIV).

Like Gideon, we listen to the wrong voices, bow to the wrong audience, and diligently catalog flimsy excuses in hopes of escaping whatever step of faith God asks us to take. In doing so, we miss the highest blessings He has to offer.

I want it all! I want everything God has for me! I don't want to miss a single step on my journey to the heart of God. I want to be the woman God created and now calls me to be—but how? The life of Gideon offers five steps we can take in order to recognize and perceive our worth in the eyes of God.

Step One: Understand That We Are Chosen

Situational ethics is now being taught in many of our public schools. One teacher, wanting to illustrate that human reasoning is many times wrong, gave the following situation to a class of high school students: "How would you advise a mother who was pregnant with her fifth child, based on the following facts: Her husband had syphilis, and she had tuberculosis. Their first child was born blind, the second child died. A third child was born deaf, while their fourth child had tuberculosis. The mother is considering an abortion. Would you advise her to have one?" In view of these facts, most of the students agreed that the mother should have an abortion. The teacher then announced, "If you said 'yes,' you would just have killed the great composer Ludwig van Beethoven."

You and I were created as living, fleshed-out depictions of God's love. We can celebrate the precious truth of Psalm 139:14-16:

> I praise you because you made me in an amazing and wonderful way. What you have done is wonderful. I know this very well. You saw my bones being formed as I took shape in my mother's body. When I was put together there, you saw my body as it was formed. All the days planned for me were written in your book before I was one day old (NCV).

Just think of it! God Himself supervised our formation. We were created in love—for love—with a specific and holy purpose in mind. We can rejoice further with the psalmist, who also wrote, "Know that the LORD is God. He made us, and we belong to him; we are his people, the sheep he tends" (Psalm 100:3 NCV).

Many women in ministry buy into the lie that we are little more than puppets in the hands of God—that He created us as tools for His personal use or slaves to do His bidding and carry out His plan. God loves us and longs to have an intimate relationship with each one of us. It is the love-filled relationship of Father and daughter:

> When our lives are broken, when the plan falls apart and everything goes wrong, we need to wait on God, knowing He created us, knows us best, and loves us most.

> You have not received a spirit of slavery leading to fear again, but you have received a spirit of adoption as sons by which we cry out, "Abba! Father!" The Spirit Himself testifies with our spirit that we are children of God, and if children, heirs also, heirs of God and fellow heirs with

Christ, if indeed we suffer with Him so that we may also
be glorified with Him (Romans 8:15-17 NASB).

God undoubtedly has plans for us, but we misunderstand His
character and heart when we assume those plans serve as a punishment or penalty for not being good enough. Jeremiah understood
the heart of God toward His children when he wrote, "'I know
what I am planning for you,' says the LORD. 'I have good plans for
you, not plans to hurt you. I will give you hope and a good future'"
(Jeremiah 29:11 NCV). The best plan, the highest plan for our lives
rests in the hands of the One who created us.

In the early days of the automobile, a man's Model-T Ford stalled
in the middle of the road. No matter what he tried, he couldn't get
it started. A chauffeured limousine pulled up behind him, and a
wiry, energetic man stepped from the backseat to offer his assistance.
After tinkering with the engine for a few moments, the stranger said,
"Now try it!" Immediately, the engine leaped to life. The man then
identified himself as Henry Ford. "I designed and built these cars,"
he said, "so I know what to do when something goes wrong." When
our lives are broken, when the plan falls apart and everything goes
wrong, we need to wait on God, knowing He created us, knows us
best, and loves us most. We are chosen, just like Gideon.

Gideon was a farmer, a family man just trying to earn a living
and put food on the table. Like us, he felt inadequate and unworthy of God's choice. But God saw what he would become, not just
what he was. The angel called him a "mighty warrior," a title that's
almost laughable because Gideon certainly didn't look like a mighty
warrior nor did he act like one. Therefore, the only explanation or
reason he could possibly become a mighty warrior was because the
Lord would be with him. He was chosen. The only reason we can
experience power in ministry is because we are chosen by God.

Step Two: Be Honest About Weaknesses

When our son, Jered, began to walk, I immediately noticed his
feet turned inward. Our pediatrician recommended a specialist,

who examined Jered thoroughly, then ordered several X-rays. The more he examined Jered, the more concerned we became. When he finally called us in for a consultation, we braced ourselves for bad news…just in case. The doctor's face revealed nothing, but his diagnosis was a gift. "There is nothing wrong with Jered's feet," he said. "They are simply the feet of a natural athlete and were designed to give him great balance." What we feared as weakness, an obstacle to overcome, was in reality a great strength and part of the Master plan for Jered, who now attends college on a football scholarship.

The same is true in our lives as children of God and women in ministry. We were created by God, according to His plan, in love and with purpose—weaknesses and all. As women in ministry, we tend to view our weaknesses as liabilities. However, since our worth does not depend upon us in any way, we can and must be honest about our weaknesses, knowing they do not diminish our value in the heart and mind of God but can, in fact, become the areas through which God does His greatest work.

Instead, though, we try to ignore weaknesses, hoping no one will notice. We live in denial, assigning blame to others when we fail. Eventually, we attempt to bury our weaknesses—only to find them resurrecting themselves when we least expect it. A powerful ministry embraces pain, brokenness, and weakness and understands that perfection is for heaven, not Earth. The words of Paul express this profoundly: "God chose the foolish things of the world to shame the wise; God chose the weak things of the world to shame the strong" (1 Corinthians 1:27 NIV).

Gideon is a great example of someone who used his weaknesses as an excuse for disobedience. His threshing wheat in a winepress reflected both his fear of discovery by his enemies, the Midianites, as well as the fact that his harvest was small. Normally, wheat was threshed in an open area—on a threshing floor by oxen pulling threshing sledges over the stalks. Gideon bristled against God's direction: "My clan is the weakest…and I am the least." At first glance, this objection may have stemmed from typical Near-Eastern humility, but it may also have reflected a stark reality. The Midianites were nomadic invaders of great number and formidable strength. God wanted Gideon to defeat them, freeing the Israelites. Gideon's response was so human, and so like our own when God calls us to do something that makes little sense and seems impossible.

When we are honest about our weaknesses, we are conceding the fact that only God can accomplish anything good in or through us. God's power is instantly recognizable in obvious weakness. Just like God was with the flawed Gideon, He is with us. "God has said, 'Never will I leave you; never will I forsake you.' So we say with confidence, 'The Lord is my helper; I will not be afraid. What can man do to me?'" (Hebrews 13:5-6 NIV). God's commitment *to* Gideon reaffirmed His presence *with* Gideon and the ease with which Gideon would have victory over the Midianites.

God promised Gideon, "You will strike down all the Midianites together." The literal translation of "together" is "as if they were but one man." I love it! Here was Gideon, probably the last man anyone would choose to face the Midianites, and God is telling him the victory will be so easy it will seem like he is facing one man instead of an army of fierce invaders. Nevertheless, Gideon's attitude was lousy! I can almost hear him whining as he blamed God for getting the Israelites into their current mess and voicing major doubts about God's willingness or even His desire to save them. Still, God said he was the man for the job.

The Lord Comes Through in Our Weakness

I am constantly amazed at the way God works in my life. He constantly puts me in situations that are so over my head and beyond my ability that His presence and power are my only hope and the only possible explanation. As a high-school senior, I began taking organ lessons from our church organist. I had played the piano for years but never touched the organ, which requires an entirely different technique. I had a grand total of eight one-hour lessons under my belt when the phone call came. "Mary, we have a countywide crusade coming up in two months and would like for you to play the organ."

My first thought was that one of my friends was playing a joke on me, so I went along with the charade. "Why certainly! I can easily handle that. After all, I *have* had eight whole organ lessons. Just tell me when and where, and I'll be there with bells on!" I cheerfully replied. The jokester hesitated for a moment but went on to explain there would be at least 2000 people attending the crusade, which would be led by a well-known Texas evangelistic team. Right! "We're planning on a choir of 100 as well as soloists from across the state to sing each night. You will need to accompany both. In addition, we will need music before and during the services. Can you do it?" I still couldn't quite place the voice, but I quickly responded, "No problem," and thanked him for "the wonderful opportunity."

After hanging up, I had a good laugh and began calling friends to see who the prankster was. No one confessed, so I decided to wait them out. The next Sunday, our pastor stepped up to the pulpit to make a special announcement. "You don't want to miss a single night of the crusade," he said. "I am proud to announce that our very own Mary Parr will be playing the organ, and I know you will all want to be there to support her." My life flashed before my eyes. As I broke out in a cold sweat, my organ teacher tapped me on the shoulder, beaming, and said, "I am so proud of your courage!" Courage, nothing! We're talking sheer, unadulterated stupidity and life-threatening terror! I thought I was going to throw up or faint and prayed for death, my only way out!

Obviously, the pastor was not joking. I really had agreed to play the organ for a countywide crusade being held in the Brownwood, Texas, coliseum, and now that the entire world knew, there was no way to escape without being totally humiliated! When the ringing in my ears subsided and I could almost breathe again, panic replaced terror as I prayed the most desperate prayer of my life! *God, are you kidding me? Surely You can't be serious! This is a big mess, a colossal mistake. Help me!* Slowly but surely, a sweet peace settled my heart as I heard Him say, *Just trust me and walk through your fear.* I did.

Every day for the next two months, I spent every spare minute practicing that organ. I prayed and practiced some more. My organ teacher worked with me and assured me I could do it. The crusade began, and I quickly discovered that God specializes in the impossible. Night after night, I played songs I shouldn't have been able to play. But what amazed me most was how much fun I had playing for that crusade.

To this day, I still have no idea how God pulled it off, but this I do know—it was Him all the way! Over the years, when I've been tempted to sidestep obedience by pointing out my inadequacies and listing all of the reasons I can't do something God has asked me to do, I remember that crusade and how He came through. Nothing is impossible or out of reach when you factor Him into the equation. Still, we are often guilty of trying to convince Him that our weaknesses exempt us from walking by faith and not by sight. We are not alone.

Noah got drunk.
Abraham was too old.
Isaac was a daydreamer.
Jacob was a liar.
Leah was ugly.
Joseph was abused.
Moses had a stuttering problem.
Gideon was afraid.
Sampson had long hair and was a womanizer.
Rahab was a prostitute.
Jeremiah and Timothy were too young.
David had an affair and was a murderer.
Elijah was suicidal.
Isaiah preached naked.
Jonah ran from God.
Naomi was a widow.
Job went bankrupt.
John the Baptist ate bugs.
Peter denied Christ.

The disciples fell asleep while praying.
Martha worried about everything.
The Samaritan woman was divorced, more than once.
Zaccheus was too small.
Paul was too religious—and Lazarus was dead!

God has always allowed man's weakness to validate man's immeasurable need of His redemption and His sufficiency. He can and will use us if we allow Him to do so. We are not the message—just the messenger. Our weaknesses are not excuses to escape God's plan but divinely appointed opportunities for that plan to work.

Step Three: Choose to Face Fear

When we fail to understand and recognize our worth, fear steps in, holding us hostage. Dreams are consigned to the realm of impossibilities, and faith is paralyzed. Purpose vanishes, and uncertainty rushes in to fill the void. When dealing with fear, we must be careful not to leave God out of our thinking. Joshua didn't. He believed God when he was told, "Yes, be bold and strong! Banish fear and doubt! For remember, the Lord your God is with you wherever you go" (Joshua 1:9 TLB). Joshua's job consisted of leading more than two million people into a strange new land and conquering it. What a challenge—even for a man of Joshua's capability! Ministry is definitely a challenge. Without God, it can be a frightening trial. With God, it can be a great adventure.

Just as God was with Joshua, He is with us as we face new challenges in ministry. We may not conquer nations, but every day we face intense needs, difficult people, and daunting situations that are out of our control. God promises He will never abandon us or fail to help us. Armed with that truth, we can choose to face fear head on. We can learn to walk through fear instead of cowering in its shadow or hoping it will somehow disappear. We can choose to live beyond ourselves and elect to act against our weak character because when we step beyond our strength, we are stepping into His.

Gideon was afraid. I understand his fear, don't you? There he was, threshing wheat and minding his own business, when an angel appeared with orders that seemed totally beyond his ability! Fear reared its ugly head. Uncertainty erupted in his heart. "If the LORD is with us, why has all this happened to us? Where are all his wonders that our fathers told us about….? The LORD has abandoned us and put us into the hand of Midian. How can I save Israel? My clan is the weakest in Manasseh, and I am the least in my family."

Oh, how familiar those doubts sound. Like Gideon, my first response to a challenge is too often fear, followed closely by a list of excuses why I can't do what God has asked me to do—as if He were unaware of who I really am! God responded to Gideon with a truth that changed everything, "I will be with you, and you will strike down all the Midianites together." Gideon could not wrap his meager faith around the fact that God's presence shifts the balance of power in any fearful circumstance. He was calculating the situation as if he were God.

As women in ministry, we tend to play God. We turn to others for wisdom instead of falling on our knees, where wisdom lives. Fear is a control issue. Its opposite is trust. Playing God is the root of all fear because when we assume the role of God, we are relying upon our limited resources instead of His limitless power. The result is impotent ministry. But every opportunity to fear is also an opportunity to trust. When confronted with fear, we need to take action.

First Action: Admit Fear

When I am afraid, I put my trust in you (Psalm 56:3 NRSV).

We will never be completely free of fear this side of heaven, so it is important for us to learn how to manage fear by replacing it with trust. Notice this verse does not say "if" I am afraid, but "when" I am afraid. No fear will be conquered until it is faced, exposed, and identified. Instead, we mask fear, hoping to camouflage weakness.

We can put fear in its place by putting trust in God. Someone once told me, "Mary, no one thinks you are perfect. Give it a rest!"

I did. Freedom is found when we embrace our imperfection along with God's power.

Second Action: Commit Fear

> The LORD is my light and the one who saves me. I fear no one. The LORD protects my life; I am afraid of no one (Psalm 27:1 NCV).

Confidence in God's presence is our basic weapon against fear. In other words, give your fears to someone who can really do something about them. When our daughter, Danna, was a little girl, her two greatest fears were the dark and thunderstorms. One night, as I was putting her to bed, I heard the distant rumblings of a storm approaching. With every clap of thunder, her eyes widened in alarm. When lightning streaked across the menacing sky, she dove under the covers and began to pray: "God, if it's a 'wittle' storm, I can just stay in my bed. But if it's a 'biiiiiiig' storm, I just want You to know I'm gonna be in mama and daddy's bed! Amen." Committing our fears to God means crawling up into His lap until the storm passes.

Third Action: Remit Fear

> Cast all your anxiety on him, because he cares for you (1 Peter 5:7 NRSV).

Instead of clinging to fear, we must *remit* fear to God—or as Peter says, we cast all fear and anxiety on Him. "Cast" means "to throw on" while "anxiety" has the root meaning "to be pulled in different directions." It's similar to the old English word from which we get our word "worry," meaning "to strangle." What a perfect description of fear at work!

The Comanche Indians tortured and killed their enemies by staking them to the ground and wrapping a wet leather strip around their necks. As the leather dried, it gradually cut off their air supply, choking the victim to death. Fear strangles our dreams, but trust breaks its grip, setting us free. We can walk in that freedom, claiming it as our own.

Each year, a bazaar was held in a small village. For one week, craftsmen, artists, farmers, people from all walks of life gathered to sell their wares. One trader brought a covey of quail. In order to display the birds, he drove a wooden stake into the ground and then tied one end of a string to the stake and the other end to one leg of each bird. The birds instinctively marched in a circle around the stake.

People came and went, but no one seemed interested in buying the quail. As merchants began leaving for the day, a kindhearted man who valued life stepped into the circle of birds and said, "I'll take them all. How much do they cost?" The trader was thrilled but, knowing he still had several days to sell the birds, named an exorbitant price. The buyer paid the price and immediately instructed the man to set the birds free.

Stunned, the trader asked, "Why would you pay so much and then let the birds go free?" The buyer smiled and offered no explanation except to say, "They are mine. I bought them. I can do whatever I want with them. So, please cut the strings and set them free." The merchant shook his head in disbelief but did as the man asked. The quail kept marching in a circle until their new owner clapped his hands, startling them into flight. The birds flew a short distance, landed, and once again, marched in a circle. Though they were free, they were still living as if they were captive and utterly powerless to escape.

We yield to fear, authorizing it to hold us prisoner. We willingly position the fearful circumstance between us and God. However, our choice to face fear puts God between us and our circumstances, unleashing His power in ministry.

Step Four: Trust God Completely

The minute God spoke, Gideon began sputtering every excuse imaginable. He pointed out every obstacle, reminding God of his weakness and venting his anger and confusion while questioning the validity of God's choice. Making excuses is always a waste of time because God is completely aware of our circumstances and knows us better than we know ourselves. When He calls us, He not only equips us but empowers us to obey that calling. If we are willing, God will supply all the strength we need. "And I thank Christ Jesus our Lord who has enabled me, because He counted me faithful, putting me into the ministry" (1 Timothy 1:12 NKJV). The Lord told Gideon to "go in the strength you have." In other words, God was asking Gideon to step out in faith, knowing his meager strength would not be enough for the task ahead. Our strength is *never* enough for any ministry task. Faith is a willingness to step out in midair, no safety net in sight.

> I am convinced our Father takes heaven-sent treasures, buries them at the heart of a huge problem, then watches and applauds when we have what it takes to break that problem apart, finding the treasure hidden there in the darkness.

Have you seen the movie *Indiana Jones and the Last Crusade*? I hate that movie! The hero, Indiana Jones, is constantly hovering above some bottomless pit—or dodging bullets, flying knives, or hoards of sinister enemies and nasty creatures trying to kill him and prevent him from completing his mission. It wears me out!

One part of the movie stands out above the rest as terrifying moments go. As usual, Indiana is on the run. He comes to a chasm he must cross in order to obtain the Holy Grail. No bridge. No net. No ropes or hat tricks—just air and nothing but air. Indiana has uncovered an important clue on his journey. If he steps over the edge of the pit—in faith—the clue promises that a rock path will appear, *but* he has to step out first. Even though I have seen the movie several times, my stomach still lurches as Indiana closes his eyes, takes a deep breath, and fearfully steps into the seemingly bottomless abyss. The moment his foot is over the chasm, the promised path appears, and he races across to safety.

Gideon and Indiana Jones have a lot in common when it comes to faith. "Am I not sending you?" God asked Gideon, as if that fact explained it all. Actually, it does explain it all. In order to experience the power of God in ministry, we have to be willing to step out in faith, even when it seems there is no way and our strength is gone. God will strengthen us *as we go*. He is the Way-Maker!

The Coast Guard has a motto: "You must go out but you don't have to come back." Powerful ministry is fueled by the kind of faith that steps out in obedience and lets God worry about whether or not we come back. Paul had that kind of faith:

> My gracious favor is all you need. My power works best in your weakness. So now I am glad to boast about my weaknesses, so that the power of Christ may work through me (2 Corinthians 12:9).

At the center of every challenge is an opportunity for trust to work. Every problem contains a concentrated opportunity and offers the option of stepping out in faith.

The greatest truths God has to offer are not wrapped in a sophisticated package and handed to us on a silver platter. I am convinced our Father takes heaven-sent treasures, buries them at the heart of a huge problem, then watches and applauds when we have what it takes to break that problem apart, finding the treasure hidden there in the darkness. The words of Isaiah say it well—"I will give you treasures hidden in the darkness—secret riches. I will do this so you may know that I am the LORD, the God of Israel, the one who calls you by name" (Isaiah 45:3).

Gideon had a trust problem. Honestly, he had no idea whether or not God would come to his defense. But instead of choosing to doubt his Father, he chose to trust Him.

> They asked each other, "Who did this?" When they carefully investigated, they were told, "Gideon son of Joash did it." The men of the town demanded of Joash, "Bring out your son. He must die, because he has broken down Baal's altar and cut down the Asherah pole beside it." But Joash replied to the hostile crowd around him, "Are you going to plead Baal's cause? Are you trying to save him? Whoever fights for him shall be put to death by morn-

ing! If Baal really is a god, he can defend himself when someone breaks down his altar" (Judges 6:29-31 NIV).

It was entirely possible that Gideon's father, Joash, would have initiated the charge to execute him because his son was openly defying him. Gideon's choice to obey God meant choosing not to obey his father. He might as well have announced, "I reject your religion, your position, and everything you stand for." Only God knew what the outcome would be. Gideon did not have a clue, but what he did know was that he was responsible for making the right choice, and God was responsible for the results. God always honors the step of faith taken in the darkness.

Step Five: Run the Race for an Audience of One

If we cannot find our identity in Christ, we are likely to seek it from those who are more than willing to define us by their own inadequate standards. Ministry is filled with all kinds of crowds. Some crowds cheer us on for all of the right reasons. Others cheer us on as a power play. And of course, jeering crowds always stand ready to criticize and discourage. Trouble comes when we cater to any one of these crowds.

To experience the power of God in ministry, we cannot rely upon the support of man in any decision to obey God. At some point we will face great opposition that, as it passes through the Father's hand, will become a refining fire. If we don't understand who our audience really is, and who we really are in the eyes of man and in the eyes of God, we will crumble and fall.

> So be truly glad! There is wonderful joy ahead, even though it is necessary for you to endure many trials for a while. These trials are only to test your faith, to show that it is strong and pure. It is being tested as fire tests and purifies gold—and your faith is far more precious to God than mere gold. So if your faith remains strong after being tried by fiery trials, it will bring you much

praise and glory and honor on the day when Jesus Christ
is revealed to the whole world (1 Peter 1:6-7).

Did Gideon receive praise for his giant leap of faith and obedience? Far from it! All he heard was harsh criticism and death threats. God knows exactly what He can do through you and through me if we are willing to let Him. But don't expect others to understand, approve, cheer, or offer encouragement, because it may or may not come. The only One you can always depend on to be in your cheering section is God. He is your audience. Be willing to run the race for Him alone.

My husband, Dan, was the pastor of Flamingo Road Church in Ft. Lauderdale, Florida, for 13 years. During our first year, the church experienced explosive growth. God was doing a new work, and we were excited to be a part of it—until we discovered most of the growth was due to people coming from other churches in the area. At the time, Ft. Lauderdale was 95 percent unchurched. Dan was heartbroken when he realized we were missing our God-appointed target of pagans—men and women without God.

Grabbing his Bible, shaving kit, and a change of clothes, my husband headed to the beach for a silent retreat. When he returned three days later, I took one look at his face and knew he had indeed been with God. We stayed up most of that night talking as Dan shared the new vision God had given him. I will never forget his words, "Honey, the next few years are going to be the most exciting and most brutal years we have ever spent in ministry." I wasn't exactly sure what he meant, but I knew we both wanted what God wanted, and that was all that mattered.

We immediately discovered that change is incredibly hard, extremely personal, and always costly. God had given Dan and the pastoral team of Flamingo Road a new dream—to go after the ones nobody else wanted. God's vision meant changes of all kinds—music, worship, outreach methods, small-group Bible study, and style of leadership. As the numbers grew, we realized our growth would soon be limited by lack of space. After much prayer, the plan was made to leave our existing facility and move two miles down the road to the local high school, where we could double in size while building a new auditorium. The move would demand sacrifice, hard work, and a horde of willing volunteers.

For several months before the congregation voted on the decision to move, Dan repeatedly shared his heart and vision with the people of Flamingo Road. Midweek services included a question-and-answer time. Plans were made and bathed in fervent prayer. Of course, there were those who resisted change and openly asserted their belief that the church should remain small and friendly. Others didn't understand why we should move to a high school when we already had a building. I honestly wasn't sure how the vote would go. Dan didn't seem to be worried. "My only concern is 'making it hard to go to Hell from Ft. Lauderdale,'" he said.

On the Sunday we were to vote, Dan invited the pastors to our home for prayer. Afterward, I asked the question that had plagued me all week. "What are you going to do if they vote no?" Without hesitation, the youth pastor said, "I can work for my father-in-law." The worship leader added, "I can help Dad clean drainage pipes." Dan jumped in. "And I can teach at any of the local colleges." I was confused. My husband explained, "Honey, if they vote no, we'll resign and find people who are willing to follow the vision God has given us. We are committed. We will do whatever it takes to do what God has called us to do. He is our audience."

Thankfully, the church voted yes, and over the next 11 years, it grew from a congregation of 300 to one of 2500 (70 percent of whom were previously unchurched), started 23 mission churches, added five worship services, and transitioned from a program-driven church to a purpose-driven church. Why? A group of pastors and people were willing to run the race for an audience of One.

Our son, Jered, plays college football and is the starting fullback on his team. Dan and I don't miss a single game. In fact, we plan speaking engagements, travel schedules, and ministry commitments around those games. Every week, from the last Saturday in August through Thanksgiving, we can be found on the fifty-yard line, five rows up. We scream, cheer, yell, celebrate, and freely offer "helpful" tips to both coaches and referees. We are what you might call "enthusiastic fans" and are proud of it! In fact, I have been known to clear out all five rows in front of me during a game. I once asked Jered if he could hear me screaming in the stands, to which he quickly replied, "Mom, *everyone* can hear you screaming!" I grinned. "Great! I just wanted to make sure I was doing my job." You see, from the moment his team bursts through the cheerleaders' banner and explodes onto the football field, my eyes are focused on one player—our son. When he hits the fifty-yard line, he glances up into the stands, grins at us—then focuses all of his attention on the game before him. But he knows. Jered knows he can count on us. We will be there, cheering him on.

Our Father is always there, cheering us on as we run the race of life and get into the contest of ministry. We are His children, His heartbeat, and the apple of His eye. No matter what we face, we can rest in the promise that He is our audience—faithful and true.

I believe one of the major barriers to powerful ministry is a faulty perception of our identity in Christ. If we could catch even a glimpse of who we are in His eyes, we would never be the same. He planned us, created us, and chose us to be His own—a truth that can free us to embrace every part of our God-ordained identity, even our weaknesses. Because He loves us unconditionally, we can trust Him, knowing He stands ready to unleash His power through our lives as women in ministry.

A Creed for Life

Don't undermine your worth by comparing yourself to others.
It is because we are different that each of us is special.

Don't set your goals by what other people deem important.
Only God knows what is best for you.

Don't take for granted the things closest to your heart.
   Cling to them as you would your life,
   for without them, life is meaningless.

Don't let life slip through your fingers
   by living in the past or for the future.

By living your life one day at a time,
   you live all the days of your life.

Don't give up when you still have something to give.
   Nothing is really over until the moment you stop trying.

Don't be afraid to admit that you are less than perfect.
   It is this fragile thread that binds us to each other.

Don't be afraid to encounter risks.
   It is by taking chances that we learn to be brave.

Don't shut love out of your life
   by saying it is impossible to find.

The quickest way to receive love
   is to give love.

The fastest way to lose love
   is to hold it too tightly;

And the best way to keep love
   is to give it wings.

Don't dismiss your dreams.
   To be without dreams is to be without hope.

To be without hope
   is to be without purpose.

Don't run through life so fast that you forget
   not only where you've been,
   but also where you are going.

Life is not just a race,
   but a disciplined journey to be
   savored each step of the way.

AUTHOR UNKNOWN

How to Perceive Your Worth

Key verse: "The God who made you is like your husband. His name is the LORD All-Powerful" (Isaiah 54:5 NCV).

Key truths: When Dan and I were first married, I struggled with what to call his parents. "Mr. and Mrs. Southerland" seemed too formal, but "Jerry and Norma" seemed too familiar and did not express my level of respect for them. On the other hand, "Mom and Dad" was just a little too intimate for me—maybe because I was still working through a lot of issues concerning my dad who died when I was five years old. My mom was both mother and father to me, and it almost seemed disloyal to address another woman as "Mom".

I solved my problem by not calling them anything—which was not really a solution at all. After years of marriage, after the death of my own mother and the survival of many family crises with Dan's parents, I one day found myself calling them "Mom" and "Dad." It was not a conscious decision on my part, but it seemed perfectly natural. In fact, I did not even realize I had made the transition until Dan commented on how much it meant to them that I would call them "Mom" and "Dad." I then realized I had not only grown to love and respect them more, but my relationship with them had grown to a new, intimate level as well.

The same should be true for our spiritual journey. How can we know God in an intimate way—on the marriage level? We get to know anyone we meet by first exchanging names. I taught my children that a simple way to meet someone new is to say, "Hi! My name is Jered. What's yours?" Names are very important.

God has a first name—Yahweh (or the traditional form, Jehovah), a Hebrew word that means "I am." "Lord" should be translated "Yahweh," meaning that Yahweh Almighty is His name. English translators have usually done a great job with the Bible, but here they've taken the name of God and substituted a title for it. Therefore, when you see "LORD" in all caps (or "LORD") read it as "Yahweh." Yahweh is a personal name that reveals the very core of God's being—His sufficiency and holiness. God wants to be on a first-name basis with us and wants us to come to Him just as we are, weak and incomplete. When we come before Him, sharing who we really are and what we really need, God then shares His last name.

God's last name is always based upon the current need of our lives. God came to Moses and said, "I want you to be on a first-name basis with me. My name is 'Jehovah'"—and from that point on, whenever the people had a need, they cried out, "God, you are the I AM. Come and meet us!" God would then come, meet them, and give them His last name.

- In Exodus 16 the people cry "God, we're out here in the desert with no food or water, starving to death! Jehovah, where are You?" God says, "I'm right here. My name today is Jehovah Jireh, which means 'Provider.'" All of a sudden, quail are raining down from heaven, manna is found on the desert floor, and new water begins pouring out of a rock.

- In Exodus 17, the people come up against a vastly superior military force and cry out to God, "We can't do this! This army will wipe us out! Please help us!" God says, "I'll be there. My name today is Jehovah Nissi, which means 'Banner.'" In Biblical times, when tribes went to war, flags and banners were carried out in front. God is telling the people that He will go before them and fight the battle for them.

- In other passages, people come to God, overwhelmed and anxious. God says, "I am Jehovah Shalom, your 'Peace.'"

- David comes to Him in a moment of desolation and says, "God, I am in the wilderness totally alone." God says, "I am Jehovah Shammah. I am 'here.'"

- Jesus cries out to God, saying, "Abba, Father," which means "Dearest Daddy," a name that paints the picture of a broken-hearted child climbing up into the lap of a loving Father.

God wants an intimate "marriage level" relationship with you, His child. You can come to Him, calling Him by name and He will meet the need of your heart.

Application steps:

- Understand that you can come to God on a first-name basis.
- Accept God's invitation to meet Him at the point of your deepest need.

- Recognize that intimacy requires honesty.
- Be willing to come to Him—just like you are.

Memory verse: "Keep me as the apple of Your eye; Hide me under the shadow of Your wings" (Psalm 17:8 NKJV).

Reflection point: *We listen to the wrong voices, bow to the wrong audience, and catalog flimsy excuses in hopes of escaping whatever step of faith God asks us to take.*

Record any thoughts or fresh insights concerning the above statement:

_____

_____

_____

Power verses:

You should not be like cowering, fearful slaves. You should behave instead like God's very own children, adopted into his family—calling him "Father, dear Father" (Romans 8:15).

I will cry out to God Most High, to God who performs all things for me (Psalm 57:2 NKJV).

He who dwells in the shelter of the Most High will rest in the shadow of the Almighty. I will say of the Lord, "He is my refuge and my fortress, my God, in whom I trust" (Psalm 91:1-2 NIV).

One new truth you've realized:

_____

_____

_____

W   Worthiness
O   Only
R   Realized
T   Through
H   Him

Hey! Are You the Pastor's Wife?

A Life Story by Kelley Searcy

Kelley and Nelson Searcy *planted Journey Church of the City in New York City shortly after the September 11 tragedy. Kelley has been a pastor's wife for 11 years, frequently ministers to the wives of church planters, and is the creator of the CD* Is My Husband's Call My Call? *(See www.epicteam.org.)*

astor's wife—noun: "the first and last name of the person married to the senior pastor."

While I was shopping with a close friend, we ran into someone she knew. "This is my pastor's wife, Kelley," she offered. She didn't say, "Please meet my good friend, Kelley" or "my friend, Kelley, who happens to be my pastor's wife." She introduced me as the pastor's wife.

Now don't get me wrong. I love being a pastor's wife. In fact, there is no one I would rather be married to, nor is there any other role I would rather play. But I have always struggled with the fact that the title of "pastor's wife" puts me in a box I sometimes find uncomfortable. I cannot think of another profession that is defined quite like the pastorate. Why is the calling to ministry so different? How can we embrace that calling?

Realize We Are Not Alone

Thankfully, God not only loves us but is faithful to us. "Be strong and courageous. Do not be afraid...for the LORD your

God goes with you; he will never leave you nor forsake you" (Deuteronomy 31:6 NIV).

While I know that God is with me and will never leave me, I must admit I have experienced times of great loneliness in ministry. I long for intimate fellowship with other women. A great mentor once told me I should strive to have three types of friendships: playmates, peers, and personal confidantes.

Playmates are those you just have fun with—the friends you get a pedicure with on a Saturday afternoon or laugh with on a girl's night out. You simply enjoy life with playmates.

Peers are other ministry wives with whom you can share the good, the bad, and the ugly, knowing they will understand because they are experiencing it, too.

Personal confidantes are the hardest friends to find. In fact, I am still struggling with this one. These women are friends you can "throw up" on. They will not only clean up the mess, but they'll never tell anyone you were sick. Make sure personal confidantes are trustworthy and committed to you. Pray for discernment and direction in finding them.

Reaffirm Your Call

I believe God calls both husband and wife into ministry. There is no doubt in my mind that I am called to be the pastor's wife at Journey Church of the City in New York. Sometimes, though, we equate God's call with an easy life. We think, since God called us, every piece in the ministry puzzle will simply fall into place. I have found just the opposite is true. The more successful I am at living out God's call for my life, the more spiritual opposition I face—betrayed confidences, marital tension, and loss of excitement. Satan doesn't always attack my weaknesses. He sometimes targets my strengths instead. There have been times in ministry when I have been frustrated and discouraged to the point of giving up. In those moments, I remember God's call and celebrate the fact we really are making a difference. My greatest affirmation is the new believer. Every time someone makes a commitment to Christ, I think, *Because I was true to who God called me to be, these people came to know Christ.*

Revel in Your Uniqueness

God made us in His image, but as Paul says in Romans 12:4-13, God designed us in such a way that it takes all of us working together to build His kingdom. Revel in the fact that God not only chose you for ministry, but that He uniquely shaped you for your role in that ministry.

I have sometimes felt inadequate because I don't fit what I see as the "traditional pastor's wife" role. I don't sing, play the piano, or know how to cook. I chose a career over staying at home. In my eyes, I was the antithesis of what a pastor's wife should be. It has taken time for me to be comfortable as a woman in ministry. More importantly, I have become comfortable being the person God called me to be. How has God shaped you for ministry? Here are some questions to start the process:

- What are my spiritual gifts? (See Romans 12; 1 Corinthians 12; Ephesians 4.) If you are unclear about your gifts, purchase a spiritual-gifts assessment at your local Christian bookstore or online.

- What is my heart passion? (Do you like to work with children? Do you have a heart for unwed mothers or the homeless?)

- What are my talents? Focus on those abilities and talents you enjoy and are good at. (If you are good at sewing but hate to do it, don't list it.)

- What is my personality type? An introvert or extrovert? A dreamer or detail person? (The DISC, Discover Your Personality by Gary Smalley, and the Myers-Briggs are great personality assessment tools.)

- What have I experienced that might help someone else? Record your life experiences—both good and bad—that have impacted your life.

Finding my niche in ministry is an ongoing process. I will be content in my role as a pastor's wife only if I am true to the person God created me to be. There is no greater adventure in life than building the kingdom of God. Wake up every morning asking, "How can you use me today, God, as a woman in ministry?"

Unleash Your Faith

iracles should be a daily occurrence. "God-things" should be the norm if we truly know and abide in Christ. Men and women leave ministry every day, their lives shattered by the hammer blows of ministry life. Ministry done in human power is consuming and futile. Ministry done in God's power is powerful and life-changing.

We cannot lead where we have not been, we cannot share what we do not possess, and we cannot convey a message of power from a powerless life. God stands ready to pour His power into us and then through us to a world filled with hurting, wounded, and hopeless people. All of His power is at our disposal, yet we are often satisfied to work day in and day out in a miracle-less ministry filled with results that can be understood in human terms. I desperately want to minister in such a way that one day, I can look back in wonder at all of the "God-things" He did in and through my life. I pray that those who come behind me will celebrate me for an ordinary life that was lived in extraordinary ways and was explainable only through a power man can neither produce nor comprehend—God's power.

The power of God is unleashed through faith. Faith is a personal issue. Just as we cannot inherit or borrow faith, neither can we rely on the faith of anyone else. We must have our own faith.

As a freshman in college, I began dating a young man whose faith was very different from my own. Normally, I would never have considered dating anyone whose beliefs were in such stark contrast to mine, but we had so many other things in common and so enjoyed being together that we decided to take the risk and just date for fun. Big mistake! Neither one of us was prepared for the fact that our relationship would quickly escalate into a serious one, but we both realized that unless we resolved the faith issue, we would never have a future together.

I had attended church from birth and simply assumed that my beliefs were right because they were all I knew—until someone questioned the authenticity of my commitment to God. I began to examine my faith and ended up making it my own. While a human relationship ended, I will be forever grateful that God used that young man to affirm my belief system, test my faith, and deepen my eternal relationship with Him.

Ministry is no place for the faithless. A powerful ministry is built upon and flows from a faith firmly rooted in God. It takes an unyielding faith to withstand the demands and tests of being in ministry. It always has.

> By faith Abraham, when God tested him, offered Isaac as a sacrifice (Hebrews 11:17 NIV).

> It was by faith that Isaac blessed the future of Jacob and Esau. It was by faith that Jacob, as he was dying, blessed each one of Joseph's sons...It was by faith that Joseph, while he was dying, spoke about the Israelites leaving Egypt and gave instructions about what to do with his

body. It was by faith that Moses' parents hid him for three months after he was born…It was by faith that Moses, when he grew up, refused to be called the son of the king of Egypt's daughter (Hebrews 11:20-24 NCV).

It was by faith that Moses left Egypt and was not afraid of the king's anger…It was by faith that Moses prepared the Passover and spread the blood on the doors so the one who brings death would not kill the firstborn sons of Israel. It was by faith that the people crossed the Red Sea as if it were dry land. But when the Egyptians tried it, they were drowned. It was by faith that the walls of Jericho fell after the people had marched around them for seven days. It was by faith that Rahab, the prostitute, welcomed the spies and was not killed with those who refused to obey God (Hebrews 11:27-31 NCV).

The Bible is filled with men and women whose lives and ministries exemplified a stellar faith. Peter is one of my favorites. I know what you are thinking. With all of the faithful saints who have gone before us, surely I could have picked a better example of faith than the man who doubted God and denied Jesus. In fact, most people would say that Peter's life is the perfect example of a weak faith. As I studied Peter, I discovered that my own faith parallels his in many ways. The similarities especially hit home as I read Peter's experience of walking on the water to Jesus.

Jesus said, "Bring the bread and the fish to me." Then he told the people to sit down on the grass. He took the five loaves and the two fish and, looking to heaven, he thanked God for the food. Jesus divided the bread and gave it to his followers, who gave it to the people. All the people ate and were satisfied. Then the followers filled twelve baskets with the leftover pieces of food. There were about five thousand men who ate, not counting women and children. Immediately Jesus told his followers to get into the boat and go ahead of him across the lake. He stayed there to send the people home. After he had sent them away, he went by himself up into the hills to pray. It was late, and Jesus was there alone. By this time, the boat was already far away from land. It was being hit by waves, because the wind was blowing against it. Between three and six o'clock in the morning, Jesus came to them, walking on the water. When his followers saw him walking on the water, they were afraid. They said, "It's a ghost!" and cried out in fear. But Jesus quickly spoke to them, "Have courage! It is I. Do not be afraid." Peter said, "Lord, if it is really you, then command me to come to you on the water." Jesus said, "Come." And Peter left the boat and walked on the water to Jesus. But when Peter saw the wind and the waves, he became afraid and began to sink. He shouted, "Lord, save me!" Immediately Jesus reached out his hand and caught Peter. Jesus said, "Your faith is small. Why did you doubt?" After they got into the boat, the wind became calm. Then those who were in the boat worshiped Jesus and said, "Truly you are the Son of God!" (Matthew 14:18-33 NCV).

While I have never actually tried walking on water, life has certainly found me in a variety of "rocking boats" from time to time. As a woman in ministry, I am very familiar with high winds, pounding waves, frightening storms, and a seemingly absent God. Like Peter, I have faltered and failed, sinking in doubt and fear. But just like Jesus rescued Peter, He has repeatedly rescued me and in the process, taught me some amazing truths about faith.

Truth Number One: Faith Believes God

If your faith is not strong, you will not have strength enough to last (Isaiah 7:9 NCV).

Our ministry may be deemed successful and powerful by man's standards, but when it comes to faith, only an eternal perspective and a holy standard will do. Authentic faith produces authentic power. Faith is active—never idle. We talk a lot about faith, but the real question is, Do we live it? In his book *Holy Sweat,* Tim Hansel shares the following story of faith.

> One day, while my son Zac and I were out in the country, climbing around in some cliffs, I heard a voice from above me yell, "Hey, Dad! Catch me!" I turned around to see Zac joyfully jumping off of a rock straight at me. He had jumped and then yelled, "Hey, Dad!" I became an instant circus act, catching him. We both fell to the ground. For a moment after I caught him, I could hardly talk. When I found my voice again, I gasped in exasperation: "Zac! Can you give me one good reason why you did that?" He responded with remarkable calmness: "Sure…because you're my Dad." His whole assurance was based on the fact that his father was trustworthy. He could live life to the hilt because I could be trusted.*

The kingdom of God is to be lived, not just discussed. The faith by which we minister should be undeniable proof that God is alive and well. Let's look at this idea more closely.

Faith Believes God Is Who He Says He Is!

> Jesus said, "Bring the bread and the fish to me." Then he told the people to sit down on the grass. He took the five loaves and the two fish and, looking to heaven, he thanked God for the food. Jesus divided the bread and gave it to his followers, who gave it to the people. All the people ate and were satisfied. Then the followers filled twelve baskets with the leftover pieces of food. There

---

* Tim Hansel, *Holy Sweat* (Waco, TX: Word Books, 1987), pp. 46–47.

were about five thousand men there who ate, not counting women and children (Matthew 14:18-21 NCV).

Weak faith is not quite sure that God really is God. Did Peter
believe Jesus was who He said He was? It is interesting to notice
where Peter was before he stepped into that boat. He was with Jesus
in the middle of a miracle. Jesus had just learned that His disciple
and friend, John the Baptist, had been murdered by King Herod.
Needing time alone, Jesus "left in a boat and went to a lonely place
by himself," but when He arrived, crowds of people had gathered
to meet Him. Setting aside his own needs, Jesus had compassion on
the people and healed those who were sick.

When evening came, the disciples, realizing they were out in the
middle of nowhere, with no restaurants, no homes, and no food,
urged Jesus to send the people home to eat. Jesus had another plan
in mind. He told the disciples to feed the people. Their response
was faithless. "But we have only five loaves of bread and two fish."

At this point, it's important to realize that these very same men
had personally witnessed Jesus perform miracle after miracle. He
had healed the sick, made the blind see, and the lame walk. He
had calmed a storm, raised a young girl from the dead, convinced
demon-possessed pigs they could fly, and then empowered the disciples to perform the same kind of miracles He had performed before
their very eyes. There's more. Jesus had healed Peter's mother-in-law.
And still, the disciples didn't fully believe that God really was God.

Jesus took the five loaves of bread and two fish, blessed them,
and turned the meager snack into a feast for well over 10,000
people. Scripture tells us that Jesus then told the disciples to get in
the boat while He dismissed the lingering crowd and went to the
mountainside to pray. I believe He prayed, not only in response to
John's death, but for His disciples.

When the boat was about four miles from shore, a storm sprang
up. Even though these men were experienced fishermen and no
strangers to storms, a small boat on stormy seas is terrifying and

dangerous. I imagine the disciples were more afraid of the unknown than the storm. Yes, Jesus had sent them into the storm. Why? Perhaps He was setting the stage for another faith-building miracle, proving once again that God really is who He says He is.

Faith Believes That God Is Able

> The boat was already far away from land. It was being hit by waves, because the wind was blowing against it (Matthew 14:24 NCV).

You would think that, after seeing Jesus in action, the disciples would not let something like a little storm rock their world. They should have known with absolute assurance that God was aware of and able to meet their every need. Faith is a quiet certainty that God keeps His promises.

In ministry, we don't like to wait on God with "quiet certainty." We see a need, and instead of seeking God's wisdom and timing, we make a plan we think will meet that need and then, with earthly resources, we see that the plan is executed. As a result, we often settle for so much less than God had in mind. "Now glory be to God! By his mighty power at work within us, he is able to accomplish infinitely more than we would ever dare to ask or hope" (Ephesians 3:20). Many children seem to possess the "quiet certainty" that God is able. The prayer life of a child is often powerful as they dare to pray big prayers, asking God to do the impossible.

> We see a need, and instead of seeking God's wisdom and timing, we make a plan we think will meet that need and then, with earthly resources, we see that the plan is executed. As a result, we often settle for so much less than God had in mind.

Christmas was just around the corner when we decided to go home for the holidays. We were living in South Florida then and rarely had the opportunity or finances to fly to Texas, where Dan and I were both raised and our families still lived. Everyone was excited, especially Jered and Danna. While they looked forward to seeing all of their aunts, uncles, grandparents, and cousins, they were more excited about seeing snow for the first time. The only problem was, snow was not in the forecast. In fact, it was supposed to be unusually warm. Danna and Jered would not be deterred. Nothing we said convinced them there would be no snow for Christmas. Every night they prayed, asking God to let it snow in Texas. They told all of their friends and anyone who would listen that they were going to Texas for Christmas and that it was going to snow. I gave up, planning what I would say to Jered and Danna when it did not snow. Yes, it would be a hard lesson, but life is filled with hard lessons.

Our plane landed, and we were met with hugs and kisses from my sister and brother-in-law...but no snow. It didn't matter. Jered and Danna were ready. Betty and Carey fielded a barrage of "snow questions" as we claimed our baggage and started home. Interestingly enough, it did seem colder the closer we got to Fort Worth. In fact, by the time we arrived, it was just plain cold. But certainly not cold enough to snow.

As Dan and I unpacked suitcases, the kids squealed with delight at the Christmas tree, the gifts underneath, the home-made fudge... and the snow! "Everybody, come see the snow!" they shouted. Dan and I looked at each other, smiled, and continued unpacking, realizing that it was time for the "sometimes God says no" conversation.

Suddenly, my usually rational sister appeared in the doorway of our bedroom, eyes big as saucers. "You are not going to believe this!" she said. The kids had obviously convinced her to help with the charade. Dan and I played along, following her to the living room—where both Jered and Danna were plastered against the sliding glass door, watching giant snowflakes gently fall, their faith on display for all to see.

Over the years I have often relived that moment, cherishing the lesson I learned that day. God is able! Even when everything seems wrong and everyone shouts "impossible," He is able. We may not always understand the process, but we can always rest in the fact that God is God, able to meet every need in ways we cannot begin to imagine outside the possibilities of true faith.

Faith Believes That God Is Willing

> Between three and six o'clock in the morning, Jesus came to them, walking on the water (Matthew 14:25 NCV).

Many women in ministry say they *do* believe God is who He says He is and that He *is* able to do what He says He will do, but they falter at the point of believing that He is *willing* to work in their lives and ministries. If we don't believe God is willing to keep His promises, we are not walking in faith. Oh, we readily teach and find it easy to agree mentally with the truth that we serve a powerful God who loves us and has a great plan for our lives, but that belief is worthless until it settles into our hearts and changes the way we live. If we don't live it, we don't really believe it.

A story is told of Will Rogers. He came to his friend, the vaudevillian Eddie Cantor, for advice. Will wanted to make some important changes in his act but was worried about the danger of such changes, explaining he wasn't sure if they would work. Cantor's response was, "Why not go out on a limb? That's where the fruit is!" The same is true of faith.

Jesus came to the disciples, walking on the water, between three and six o'clock in the morning, the darkest time of the night. I have often wished I could have been on that boat with the disciples, waiting for Jesus to show up. I imagine the questions and complaints were flying! "Why would Jesus send us out here, knowing the waves were high? Where is He? Why is He waiting so long to rescue us? Can't He just calm the waves like He did before? I ministered all day long, and *this* is my reward? Is He really coming? I don't understand!" Sound familiar?

We are quick to believe the lie that God is angry with us and, as a result, will not bless our ministry or meet our needs. The truth is, God is willing and waiting to pour out His favor and blessings on a life and ministry of faith. Hebrews tells us that faith always honors

God and God always honors faith. "Without faith no one can please God. Anyone who comes to God must believe that he is real and that he rewards those who truly want to find him" (Hebrews 11:6 NCV).

Truth Number Two: Faith Can Be Unleashed

Authentic faith naturally produces action, but faith is hindered when we refuse to obey God. It is said that the African impala can jump to a height of more than ten feet and cover a distance greater than thirty feet in one jump. Yet these magnificent creatures can be kept in any zoo by a three-foot wall, it is further said, because they will not jump if they cannot see where their feet will land.

Faith is the ability to trust what we cannot see. John Shedd says, "A ship in harbor is safe, but that is not what ships are for." We fear the outcome or don't understand the step He has asked us to take. We are afraid to fail and are more concerned about our "reputation" as women in ministry than we are about being women of God. Faith is willing to take risks, embrace the unseen, and move away from the safety of the shore. But as long as the enemy can keep us preoccupied with a selfish perspective, our faith is impotent. How can we unleash the faith of God in our lives?

Prayer Unleashes Faith

> Is any one of you in trouble? He should pray…Is any one of you sick? He should call the elders of the church to pray over him…And the prayer offered in faith will make the sick person well; the Lord will raise him up… The prayer of a righteous man is powerful and effective (James 5:13-16 NIV).

A small country town was in desperate need of rain. One Sunday morning, the pastor of the local church called for a special prayer meeting to be held that night. "It's time to pray for rain," he said. The people gathered with a sense of purpose and excitement, but when the pastor stood to lead the prayer time, his words stunned the waiting crowd. "Only one of you came in faith," he announced. Looking down at the first row, the pastor pointed at a little girl who sat quietly, a smile on her face and an umbrella in her hand. We can pray for rain, but faith brings an umbrella. Prayer invites and expects God to step in and take charge. Rick Warren, the pastor of Saddleback Church in California and author of *The Purpose-Driven Life,* is a precious friend. I once asked him, "Rick, why do you think God blesses your life and this ministry in such powerful ways?" His answer was surprisingly simple: "Because I expect Him to." Prayer shuts out fear and fuels faith.

> Until we are utterly helpless, prayer seems like an option instead of our only hope.

When the winds picked up and the waves grew larger on the Sea of Galilee, I am sure every disciple in that rocking boat was praying like crazy! Unfortunately, it often takes a crisis to drive us to our knees in prayer. I think I know why. Until we are utterly helpless, prayer seems like an option instead of our only hope.

Three ministers were discussing which position produces the most powerful prayer. As they were talking, a telephone repairman was working quietly in the background. One minister shared he felt the key to powerful prayer was in the hands. He always held his hands together and pointed them upward as a symbol of worship. The second suggested real prayer was conducted on the knees, while the third minister suggested they both had it wrong. According to him, the only prayer position worth its salt was stretched out flat on your face in humility. The phone man then couldn't resist offering his opinion. "I have found the most powerful prayer I ever prayed was while I was suspended 40 feet above the ground, dangling upside down by my heels from a power pole." Helplessness underlines our need for faith, our total dependence upon God, even when the skies are clear and the water is calm.

Answered prayer should be the norm. Prayer should be as natural and as constant as breathing. A woman overheard her daughter-in-law talking on the telephone to a friend who had called, asking for prayer. Five-year-old Amy, the woman's granddaughter, came bouncing into the room, stood still for a moment to listen, and heard her mother praying. "Is that God on the phone, Mom?" she interrupted. "I need to talk to Him, too!"

Samuel Chadwick writes, "The one concern of the devil is to keep Christians from praying. He fears nothing from prayer-less studies, prayer-less work and prayer-less religion. He laughs at our toil, mocks at our wisdom, but he trembles when we pray." The best time for prayer isn't found. It's made. The average Christian woman spends very little time in prayer—then wonders why she has no faith and experiences no power. If we are too busy to pray, we are too busy to experience the power of God in ministry. We can be very busy but not necessarily productive, because we lack faith. One of the main reasons we lack faith is because we don't pray. Consistent prayer builds consistent faith.

Obedience Unleashes Faith

> Jesus said, "Come." And Peter left the boat and walked on the water to Jesus (Matthew 14:29 NCV).

It is not enough to pray. We must put obedient feet to those prayers. Faith *comes* as we *go!* The story has been told many times of the old man trapped by a flood. He was up to his knees in fast-rising waters when a rowboat came to his aid. "Hop in, we'll save you!" shouted the rescuers. "No thanks," replied the man. "The Lord will provide."

A short while later a motorboat came to save him. By this time, the swirling waters were up to his waist, still quickly rising. Again, he declined the offer. "No thanks, the Lord will provide."

Soon the water was up to his chin, so a helicopter was dispatched. The pilot shouted, "Climb aboard, sir. This is your last chance!" Once again, the old man responded, "Thanks anyway, but the Lord will provide."

Well, the old man drowned and arrived at the Pearly Gates. Furious, he bitterly complained to St. Peter, "The last thing I remember, I was in trouble, praying up a storm. Why did you let me drown?"

St. Peter looked at him and shook his head. "We sent you two boats and a helicopter. What more do you want?"

When we know the truth, we have knowledge—but when we act on the truth, we have faith. Obedience unleashes faith.

Truth Number Three: Faith Is Willing to Forsake the Known

> Peter said, "Lord, if it is really you, then command me to come to you on the water." Jesus said, "Come." And Peter left the boat and walked on the water to Jesus (Matthew 14:28-29 NCV).

Faith demands a willingness to give up what we can see for what we cannot see. "Faith is the substance of things hoped for, the evidence of things not seen" (Hebrews 11:1 NKJV). This verse carries the idea of persuasion or a conviction in response to unseen evidence. In other words, just because we can't see it, doesn't mean it isn't there.

John Paton and his wife were missionaries in the New Hebrides Islands. One night, hostile natives surrounded the mission headquarters, intent on burning the Patons out and killing them both. Paton and his wife prayed all night, asking God to strengthen their faith. At dawn, they were amazed to see their attackers simply turn and leave!

A year later, the chief of that tribe became a Christian. Paton asked him what had kept him and his men from killing them that night. The chief answered with a question: "Who were all those men you had there with you?" Paton answered, "There was no one with us. My wife and I were all alone." The chief reported they had seen hundreds of men standing guard, big men in shining garments with drawn swords. (Sounds like angels to me!) God is not only able to answer our prayer of faith, He delights in doing so.

As a fisherman, Peter knew all about boats and storms. However, I feel safe in saying that Peter had probably never tried walking on any kind of water, much less stormy water. It didn't matter. Jesus said, "Come." There is so much wrapped up in that single word. Strength for every trial, faith for every storm, courage for every conflict, the promise of His presence, and everything we need to obey is promised to those who are willing to leave the safety of the boat and "come" to Jesus.

I love the simple promise of 1 Thessalonians 5:24: "Faithful is He who calls you, and He also will bring it to pass" (NASB). God will never force or shove us into obedience, but instead, simply invites us to obey. Peter accepted the invitation of Jesus when he slipped off his sandals, hitched up his robe, and climbed over the side of that boat in sheer obedience. I am certain his heart was flooded with fear and doubt, but he still stepped through his fear and doubt onto solid ground.

Anytime we walk in obedience we are on solid ground, no matter what that ground looks like. The minute his foot touched the water, Peter left the "known" behind and stepped out in a faith that pleased God.

Truth Number Four: Faith Walks Through Fear

> Between three and six o'clock in the morning, Jesus came to them, walking on the water. When his followers saw him walking on the water, they were afraid. They said, "It's a ghost!" and cried out in fear. But Jesus quickly spoke to them, "Have courage! It is I. Do not be afraid" (Matthew 14:25-27 NCV).

As a young child, our daughter, Danna, was afraid of the dark. When I asked her why, her response was profound: "because you don't know what's hiding in it." Exactly! The darkness is the perfect hiding place for fear, doubt, insecurity, and all kinds of unseen enemies. In fact, have you noticed how rampant fear has become? I thought it would be interesting to compile a list of actual fears or phobias people struggle with. The results were amazing!

Trichopathophobia	Fear of hair disease
Teratophobia	Fear of monsters
Pteronophobia	Fear of feathers
Alektorophobia	Fear of chickens
Anglophobia	Fear of England or English
Aulophobia	Fear of flutes
Bolshephobia	Fear of Bolsheviks
Dermatosiophobia	Fear of skin
Genuphobia	Fear of knees
Phronemophobia	Fear of thinking

At some point in life we all battle fear. Fear constantly tries to elbow faith aside, hoping to derail God's plan and purpose in our lives for us as women in ministry. Fear keeps many of us from dreaming God-sized dreams, persuading us to settle for safety and comfort instead of riding the waves of holy passion. When faith yanks our hideous fears out of the darkness and into the light, we can see them for what they really are—powerless.

Faith is a three-letter word. Faith says *yes* to peace and *no* to fear. It may be one tiny step or one puny choice. It may be a whispered prayer or a desperate cry, but God always honors the choice to walk straight ahead through fear. Fear trains us to anticipate the worst, while faith teaches us to expect the best.

I have always hated wearing glasses! They get lost, slide down my nose, are always dirty, constantly have to be adjusted, and are, in general, a major nuisance. During a routine eye exam, I informed the doctor I needed contacts instead of glasses. He did not look hopeful. "Mary, you have a couple of problems that would make contacts difficult to wear." Since I did not hear the word "impossible," I was holding out for contacts! The doctor continued, "You not only have astigmatism, but your vision needs to be corrected for both distance and close vision." I tried to digest that information but was still having difficulty understanding why contacts would be a problem.

Seeing the confusion on my face, the optometrist explained I would have to wear a contact in my left eye that would allow me to see up close and a different-strength contact in my right eye that would allow me to see in the distance. "In reality," he said, "we would be tricking the brain and going against the way it was created." Since I had been doing that from birth, I still didn't see a problem. Sighing, he painted an ugly scenario. "Your brain will be confused for several months. You will step off curbs that are not there or reach for something only to knock it over. At first, you will be able to read for short periods only because your eyes will be at war over which one gets to do the job. When your brain is finally retrained, the confusion will fade, and your vision will improve greatly." I got my contacts. The first few months were indeed frustrating and difficult, but eventually my vision improved, and it seemed as though I had always worn contacts.

According to Paul, the training of the mind is not only a physical possibility but a vital spiritual principle as well:

> We fight with weapons that are different from those the world uses. Our weapons have power from God. These weapons can destroy the enemy's strong places. We destroy men's arguments. And we destroy every proud thing that raises itself against the knowledge of God. We capture every thought and make it give up and obey Christ (2 Corinthians 10:4-5 ICB).

Faith trains the mind to face and deal with fear.

The disciples were afraid. In fact, their fear blinded them from the reality of Jesus coming to them in the midst of the storm. I love His response to their fearful cries, "Have courage! It is I. Do not be afraid." Jesus did not rebuke His followers in their fear or turn away from them because their faith was weak. Jesus "quickly" assured them of His comforting presence and His available power. Peter was the only one who was willing to get out of the boat and walk through his fear. When he took that first step, Peter's fear was swallowed up in faith.

Truth Number Five: Faith Is Willing to Make a Commitment

> Trust the LORD with all your heart, and don't depend on your own understanding. Remember the LORD in all you do, and he will give you success (Proverbs 3:5-6 NCV).

Women who serve with power in ministry understand the need for commitment and are willing to pay the price it demands. A friend who works in the field of chemistry once told me if you mix hydrogen and oxygen, the two components of water, you'll get no reaction and no water. But, if you add a small amount of platinum, the hydrogen and oxygen unite and a chemical change occurs, producing H_2O. Platinum is the catalyst that produces water.

Personal commitment is the catalyst that produces personal faith. In other words, once Peter's feet touched the water, he was committed. Faith in God does not come all at once. It is a step-by-step process beginning with one small step of trust.

A grandfather was going by his little granddaughter's room one night, when he saw her kneeling beside her bed, head bowed and hands folded. As he stopped to listen, he was surprised to hear her repeating the alphabet as her prayer. Curious, he tiptoed into her room, knelt beside her, and waited for her to finish. "What are you doing?" he then asked. Smiling, the little girl explained, "I'm saying my prayers. But I couldn't think of the right words, so I'm just saying all the letters of the alphabet, and God can put them together however He wants to."

We sometimes refuse to take the first steps of faith because we're afraid we won't be able to make the whole journey. Don't wait until you believe it all! Don't wait until you can see or understand it all! Like Peter, just step out of the boat.

Truth Number Six: Faith Focuses on God

> When Peter saw the wind and the waves, he became afraid and began to sink. He shouted, "Lord, save me!" (Matthew 14:30 NCV).

I do not have a green thumb. In fact, friends and family members refuse to let me come within two feet of any living plant…but I keep trying. Recently, I planted some flowers in our front yard. Actually, I just kind of *stuck* them in the ground, prayed over them, and hoped for a miracle. After a few days, they were still alive and looking good. I was so proud! Then a summer storm came through. Afterward, I ventured outside to check on my flowers, only to discover them lying on the ground, beaten to a pulp!

> Having a personal relationship with God means that we have access to all of Him and all of His resources.

I live next door to Martha Stewart's twin sister, who had planted the very same flowers, which had gone through the very same storm. But hers were still standing tall and proud, mocking my sad, wilted floral remnants. "You didn't plant them deep enough," she sweetly explained. Evidently, the flowers were not rooted and had been easily pulled out by the storm. The same is true in our lives.

Having a personal relationship with God means that we have access to all of Him and all of His resources. A little girl ended her bedtime prayer with, "Dear God, I need You to please take care of Mommy and Daddy, take care of my sister and my brother, and please, please God, take care of Yourself because if You don't we're all sunk. Amen!" Without Him, we are indeed "sunk."

Most women in ministry would give anything to experience the peace of God. Each day brings a new list of worries, and every night is filled with "what ifs." If God authors peace, why do we often find ourselves in a constant battle against anxiety and fear? I believe it is because we are not firmly rooted in Him. We are not tapping into the vast riches that are rightfully ours as daughters of the King. We are not focused on God and His presence in our lives.

When our daughter, Danna, was in middle school, she played on a coed soccer team. During one particularly rough game, she fell, landing on her elbow. By the time I got to her, she was wailing in pain and couldn't move her fingers—not a good sign. She took one look at my face and instantly knew we were headed to the emergency room, a place she detested and feared.

On the way to the hospital, I talked up a storm, hoping to distract Danna while helping her face fear head on. "Are you scared, honey?" I finally asked. With tears streaming down her face, she looked at me and sobbed, "Yes, Mommy! I am very, very scared!" I hugged her close and said, "Danna, everything is going to be fine." A watery smile spread across her face as she responded, "I know it will be okay as long as you are there with me. Promise not to leave me, Mom." Over the years, Danna and I made several trips to the emergency room, and many more to the doctor. Every time she was terrified. Every time she made me promise to stay with her—and every time, I did. And here she was—asking…again! I could have said, "Danna! What is the matter with you? How many times have we been through this—and I never leave you, do I? When are you going to get it?" Those words never entered my mind. My baby girl was hurting. She was afraid and needed to know that she could count on me, that I would be with her—no matter what. Once again, I gladly and freely promised.

The same is true in our relationship with God. Because He is with us no matter what, we can focus on Him and walk through our fear. The deeper we delve into the truth and power of God, the stronger our personal relationship with Him will grow. Our relationship with Him will never change because He safekeeps it, but how much power we receive from Him depends upon how solid and stable that relationship is and how persistent we are in pursuing Him:

Jesus has the power of God, by which he has given us everything we need to live and to serve God. We have these things because we know him (2 Peter 1:3 NCV).

Doubt or Faith?

Peter began to sink because he doubted. He doubted because he focused on the storm instead of Jesus. To withstand the storms of life and ministry, our gaze must be on God, and our glance on the circumstances. It is a continual choice, one that will be relentlessly tested, sometimes by the very people to whom we minister or those with whom we serve. Do not allow doubters to disturb your focus.

I love the story of a farmer who had a brilliant dog. He also had a neighbor that was very negative. He doubted everyone and questioned everything. When it rained, the farmer said to his neighbor, "Boy, look at it rain. God's washing everything clean." The doubting neighbor responded, "Yeah, but if it keeps up, it's gonna flood." When the sun came out, he would say, "If it keeps that up, it's gonna burn the crops." The farmer thought, *What am I going to do to win this guy over?* Then he had an idea. He trained his dog to walk on water but didn't tell his neighbor about the dog's new ability. He just took him duck hunting at a nearby lake.

It wasn't long before shots rang out—"Boom! Boom!" Two ducks were down. "Go get those ducks, boy!" the farmer shouted. The dog sprinted across the surface of the lake, picked up the ducks, and loped back to the boat, nothing wet except the bottom of his paws. The confident farmer turned to his doubting neighbor and proudly asked, "What do you think of that?" The neighbor was silent for a moment and then shook his head. "He can't swim, can he?"

You know people like this man, don't you? It seems as if they live to challenge your faith and promote doubt in your heart. We struggle enough with our own doubt! We can't afford to compound it by spending time with doubters. Look for the people who walk in faith, and walk with them! Your faith will grow, and your doubts will die from lack of attention.

Peter cried out in fear—and it was the right thing to do! Did Jesus rebuke him? Not then. Instead of condemning his disciple, Jesus "immediately" reached out and caught him! Every time I read this passage, that word "immediately" jumps out at me. Jesus responded "immediately." He didn't say, "What a wimp! Peter knows better. I can't believe he still doubts Me. I'll just let him get wet and fend for himself! That'll teach him a lesson!" No—Jesus not only rescued His floundering disciple but walked with him the rest of the way. Jesus then corrected Peter—not because of his fear, but because Peter did not trust Him in his fear.

God's power—all of His power—is available to us. Yet we continue to minister from weakness instead of strength. Our hearts are filled with doubt instead of faith. Lives under our influence see only man-powered religious activities, when what God wants them to witness is a holy "on-the-road-to-Damascus" experience with Him. Now is the time. Unleash your faith and experience the power of God in your ministry.

How to Unleash Your Faith

Key verse: "Without faith no one can please God. Anyone who comes to God must believe that He is real and that He rewards those who truly want to find Him" (Hebrews 11:6 ICB).

Key truths: Faith is more than just believing. It is acting on that belief. The story is told of a young woman with a large family who lived in a remote valley in Wales. When electricity came to the rural area, she was one of the first customers. However, the electric company soon noticed the woman was using a very small amount of electricity each month. Suspecting a problem with the equipment, they sent a repairman to check the meter. After a close inspection, he found the equipment was installed properly. Confused, he knocked on the front door to give the woman his report. "We've inspected the meter, which seems to be working properly. The only thing I can figure out is that you're not using the power that is available. Don't you use any electricity?" "Oh, yes," she said. "We turn it on every night to see to light our oil lamps, and then we switch it off again."

As women in ministry, we often approach God's power in the same way—knowing it exists but failing to appropriate it. Instead, we work diligently in our own power. We are not saved by faith *plus* works. We are saved by faith that *leads to* good works. We attempt to build a ministry on the flawed premise that if we do enough good works, God will be pleased. However, those works are useless and count for nothing unless the heart motivation behind them is one of faith. Faith is the altar of powerful ministry.

Application steps:

- Read James 2:14. Examine your life and ministry in light of the faith James describes in this verse. Record your thoughts.
- In what area of ministry does doubt plague you most? In your personal life?
- What "God-thing" is happening in your life today?

- What steps of obedience do you need to take in order to unleash your faith?

Memory verse: "In every battle you will need faith as your shield to stop the fiery arrows aimed at you by Satan" (Ephesians 6:16).

Reflection point: *All of God's power is at our disposal, yet we are satisfied to work day in and day out in a miracle-less ministry filled with results that can be understood in human terms.*

Record any thoughts or fresh insights concerning the above statement:

_____

_____

_____

Power verses:

These trials are only to test your faith, to show that it is strong and pure. It is being tested as fire tests and purifies gold—and your faith is far more precious to God than mere gold. So if your faith remains strong after being tried by fiery trials, it will bring you much praise and glory and honor (1 Peter 1:7).

A righteous person will live by faith. But I will have no pleasure in anyone who turns away (Hebrews 10:38).

One new truth:

_____

_____

F	Forsaking
A	All
I	I
T	Trust
H	Him

My Life Story
An Interview with Katie Brazelton

Katie Brazelton, PhD, MDiv, MA, *is a licensed minister at Saddleback Church in southern California. She is the bestselling author of the Pathway to Purpose™ series for women. (Web site: www.pathwaytopurpose.com; e-mail: info@pathwaytopurpose.com.)*

1. How did God call you to ministry?

As a young girl, God called me to be His daughter. Even then, I was madly in love with the Holy Spirit. I wanted to be a "Joan of Arc" who did something great for God. When I got married and had children, I couldn't figure out how God could ever use me in a gigantic way. I was definitely more of a "Joan of Arcadia" then, just trying to hear Him on a daily basis and arguing with Him when I did hear His voice. Now, I understand how being a wife and mother is one of His callings in life.

Years later, God began to give me a sneak preview of His plan for my life. He continually talked to me about seeds that were budding and blossoming. I felt He was asking me to do something that had to do with grain, fields, pruning, or harvests—that He wanted me to help something come into full bloom for Him. I finally realized I was to nurture Christian women "seedlings": to minister to them, disciple them, and teach them to surrender their lives to God, so they would be called "oaks of righteousness, a planting of the LORD for the display of his splendor" (Isaiah 61:3 NIV). After I was hired as a staff member at Saddleback Church and was later asked to be the Director of Women's Bible Studies, a number of godly people began encouraging me to complete my seminary education and become a licensed minister at our church. As God confirmed that prompting and I prayerfully obeyed, doors flew open, and I was licensed.

2. What is your heart passion and purpose in ministry?

My passion in ministry is to give women God's gift of hope as I help them understand His unique and universal purposes for their lives. My purpose is to bring glory to God, and I believe He has designed me to do that by creating a process and providing places where women can meet with Him and others to discuss His plan for their lives. For years, I have dreamed of opening 200 Women's Life-Purpose Centers internationally, and the dream is beginning to unfold before my eyes, slowly and steadily. In preparation, I now train Christian women as Life-Purpose Coaches.

3. What has been the most rewarding part of ministry?

By far, the most rewarding part of ministry has always been helping women get *unstuck* in their personal and spiritual lives—encouraging them to leave their bitterness, regrets, fears, pain, anger, impatience, greed, jealousy, addictions, and other sins behind. For example, when a woman understands that pride is blocking her from hearing God's plan for her life, when the blinders come off as to how that sin is preventing her from ful-filling her broad-reach purpose in life, I must say that few things compare to the joy of witnessing that breakthrough.

4. What has been your greatest struggle in ministry?

My greatest struggle in ministry has been *fear*. No two ways about it—it's been the fear of its being found out that I'm not really smart enough or holy enough. My fear has been debili-tating at times and has even been a serious contributor to my bouts of depression and anxiety. I've had to choose to walk away from perfectionist tendencies that were born out of needing to outdo, outsmart, and outlast others (yes, in the past, my life has resembled a game of Survivor!).

5. *What have you learned from your struggles?*

From my struggles, I have learned I really am not smart enough or holy enough! It is only through God's mercy, grace, forgiveness, and power that I will be and do what He has in mind for me. I have learned that the secret is to surrender our lives to God. That includes our careers, finances, education, ministries, possessions, hobbies, spiritual growth, life dreams, friendships, spouses, and children, as well as our distractions, dark past, idols, and sins—just to mention a few of the biggest issues God wants us to turn over to Him.

6. *What has been the biggest surprise to you in ministry? Why?*

My biggest surprise in ministry was my negative response to several questions that had to do with how much I was willing to surrender to God. The questions were these: *Would I even love God, let alone follow him, if I lost everything—my children included? Would I love him if I became terminally ill?* It took me days of confusion, anger, and depression before I realized that everything I had, even my next breath, belonged to God. I had arrogantly forgotten that everything is *on loan* to me from the Creator of the universe. I was finally able to pray, "God...give me the grace to love You whether or not You bless my family or me. I am content with whatever You choose to bless me with or even subtract from me—my kids, eyes, hands, voice, limbs, energy, or possessions. They are all Yours, not mine."

7. *If you could share one truth with women in ministry, what would it be?*

The one truth I always share with women in ministry comes from Hebrews 11, which is all about God's faith-heroes. I love reminding women that God is drawn to our faithfulness to Him. Our persistent belief in Him, in His promises, and in His loving ways softens His heart. We need to believe prayerfully, beyond a shadow of a doubt, that God will do what He has told us He will do. Our job, while we wait on God's timing, is to trust Him and to pray persistently.

Relish Godly Discipline

rarely watch television, but I occasionally flip through channels in search of a few minutes of mindless entertainment. I especially enjoy shows featuring children in candid conversations because kids really do say the funniest things! *The Cosby Show* is one of my favorites.

I recently watched an episode where Bill Cosby's character was talking with a bright seven-year-old boy, a friend of Rudy, his daughter. "Do you have any pets?" he asked. The little boy thought for a moment and then replied, "Well, I don't have any pets now, but I used to have some goldfish." Sensing a story, Cosby's character responded, "Tell me about the goldfish. What happened?" "Well," the boy began, "my science teacher said that our water is too hard for goldfish to live in but my mom puts stuff in the washer to make our clothes soft." Moans rumbled through the audience as the little boy continued. "So...I got me some of that stuff and put it in the aquarium…but Rudy said I put too much soft stuff in, 'cause the goldfish softened to death." A lack of godly discipline in our lives renders us "soft" to the things of God. When we surrender our lives to Him, He sets our feet on the right road. To stay on that road demands godly discipline.

A Place for Rest and Trust

I am constantly amazed at the arrogance of which I am capable, daring to think I have the power within myself to intimidate Satan or thwart his efforts in my life. I have no power apart from God. I am weak without His strength, vulnerable to sin, and a prime target for temptation. As a woman in ministry, I can easily get caught up in human affirmation, my own sense of self-importance, or the flattery of others. The result is always spiritual arrogance. The solution is always godly discipline. Godly discipline is not only a hedge of protection in our lives; it is a catalyst for spiritual growth.

> Godly discipline is the basis for trust, and it's found at the feet of Jesus, where we will come to know Him better, love Him more, and receive that discipline we so desperately crave.

James Dobson says, "If one examines the secret behind a championship football team, a magnificent orchestra, or successful business, the principal ingredient is discipline."

Now I know the very word "discipline" evokes distasteful images of pain, deprivation, sacrifice, and surrender—when in fact, true discipline is simply a wholehearted "yes" to God. True discipline neither barters with God for control nor attempts to supersede His plan. Discipline does not make us worthy but is the result of understanding we are already worthy in God's eyes and then living life as a response to His love. We are chosen, loved, bought, and purchased by God, who has a sacred blueprint for each one of us. Discipline accepts that blueprint, following it with an eager obedience wrapped in sweet abandonment and absolute trust in the master plan of the Architect.

Godly discipline allows us to rest within the framework of God's sovereignty. When our son, Jered, was seven years old, he fell while skateboarding, cut his chin, and needed stitches. We raced to the nearest emergency clinic, where we were greeted by a young doctor who, at first glance, seemed friendly enough. Jered, however, took one look at the strange man in white and panicked in the midst of his first experience with stitches.

After several attempts to gain Jered's trust and cooperation, the doctor grew impatient and threatened, "Son, this won't hurt. If you cannot be still we will have to put you in restraints." This man obviously did not know who Jered was—mine—nor did he understand that he was now dealing with the wrath of Mary, something too horrible to describe. However, I was more than willing to enlighten him. I could see the warning in Dan's eyes, but chose to ignore it.

I had two major problems with the doctor's statements. First, no restraints were going to be placed on my son. Secondly, of course the stitches would hurt. Glaring at the doctor I firmly explained, "If you will just tell Jered the truth and explain what you are doing, he will be still for you." The doctor looked up at me as if I had just arrived from another planet and then, with an edge of sarcasm, spit out, "Right, lady. I know how to handle this." So did I—but before I could rip off his head, Dan intervened, telling the doctor we had a plan! I knew what *my* plan was, but I thought it wise to consider Dan's plan.

Gently holding Jered's head in his "daddy-sized" hands, Dan softly explained what the doctor would do and how he would do it, and he sweetly instructed our son to fix his eyes on me while I told him a story. It worked—of course. Jered calmed down, and the stitches were done in a matter of minutes. The doctor even offered a sheepish apology, thanking us for teaching him a lesson in working with children. I decided to let him live.

Even though Jered did not fully understand the process or trust the doctor, he did fully understand and trust his father. Godly discipline is the basis for trust, and it's found at the feet of Jesus, where we will come to know Him better, love Him more, and receive that discipline we so desperately crave.

Starting the Application

Discipline is obedience, a lifetime process that brings us to a state of God-ordained order by training and controlling our behavior. Discipline is not self-improvement, but rather placing oneself under orders. Discipline is not the result of legalism but the reward of grace. Discipline is not rigidity but flexibility, always free to respond to the plan of the Master. Discipline is focusing and eliminating, zeroing in on what is important. In fact, godly discipline becomes a buffer against sin and temptation. Titus 2:11-12 is clear on the importance of discipline in the life of every believer:

> The grace of God that brings salvation has appeared to all men. It teaches us to say "No" to ungodliness and worldly passions, and to live self-controlled, upright and godly lives in this present age (NIV).

Discipline—holding restraint in one hand and commitment in the other—is accomplished only through the power of the Holy Spirit, training and directing us in the ways of God. Our Father will neither give us good habits nor supply exemplary character. We must resolve to walk in an "upright" way. We must choose the good habits over the bad and "work out the salvation that God has worked in." We must choose and relish discipline.

The author of Proverbs offers a simple but powerful truth: "Apply your heart to instruction and your ears to words of knowledge" (Proverbs 23:12 NIV). "Apply" means to make a commitment, to decide, or to choose! When we choose to apply discipline, God empowers that choice, freeing the Holy Spirit to cultivate a spiritual control and holy order that is clearly beyond ourselves. Discipline is the mutual effort between the Holy Spirit and our will, yielded and surrendered to God's authority, mastering right attitudes and establishing right habits. The purpose of discipline is to order our lives in such a way that we are available and prepared to be used by God anywhere, anytime, and in any way.

As women in ministry, people constantly look to us for the answers to some of life's most complex questions. If our personal lives and public ministries are in chaos and out of God's control due to a lack of discipline, the answers will be buried in a sea of confusion, and we will be trapped in a deadly whirlpool of meaningless activity swarming with temptation and sin. A disciplined heart desires to please God. A powerful ministry does not stop at merely understanding discipline, but chooses to relish discipline, applying it to every area of life. How do we get there?

First, we make the commitment to start. A famous athlete, known to rise at 3:30 AM each morning to begin his demanding regimen of exercise, was being interviewed by a major newspaper. When the reporter asked him to share the secret of his success, the athlete responded, "That's easy. The secret to my success is discipline." The reporter laughed at the simplistic answer and persisted. "Yes, but how do you start leading a life of discipline?" The athlete grinned and said, "You decide to start." The same is true for us as women in ministry. A life of discipline begins with the commitment to start.

As an often-told story goes, a country preacher was visiting one of his church members, who owned a large wheat farm. As they stood, gazing out over the man's beautiful grain, the preacher commented, "Well, John, you and the Lord have done a good job on this wheat." The farmer looked thoughtfully across his field, and after a few moments he said, "Preacher, you should have seen it when the Lord had it by Himself." Godly discipline is not some lofty, ethereal attribute, but gives feet to faith and hands to obedience. Richard Foster says, "The disciplined person is someone who can do what needs to be done when it needs to be done."

*Second, we make the commitment to start **now**.* An undisciplined heart is full of good intentions that are never given life. Begin now to pursue discipline. You may not fully understand all your commitment entails, but the Holy Spirit certainly does. He will empower every well-ordered choice you make and guide every disciplined step of your journey to the heart of God. Let's go through some key steps.

First Step: Discipline My Mind

> Be very careful about what you think. Your thoughts run your life (Proverbs 4:23 ICB).

Temptation first targets the mind, knowing that thoughts determine direction. We can change our lives by changing our thought habits, by choosing to discipline our minds. As women in ministry, we should have thought lives worth recommending to others. What a haunting thought! Vulgar language, raunchy movies, questionable books, negative conversations, destructive thought patterns, ugly gossip, and disparaging criticism have no place in the life of a believer and certainly not in the heart of any woman in ministry.

These days, I am flying more and more as God opens doors for me to travel and speak. Before every flight I have to go through several security measures. I am required to show my driver's license to several hundred security personnel. My bags are rammed through an X-ray machine, and I have to answer the same set of questions about the contents of every bag. If you fly at all, you know the drill—"Are these your bags? Have they been in your possession at all times? Has anyone given you anything to carry on the plane? Please jump through this flaming hoop, prepare for a strip search, and roll up your sleeve. We need a blood sample." Well, I may have added a question or two, but it seems like a ridiculous and unnecessary ordeal…until I stop and remember that it is a lifesaving process for my good and the safety of every person on my plane. We should have this same attitude about our thought life.

In 2 Corinthians 10:5, Paul instructs us to "capture every thought and make it give up and obey Christ" (ICB). Capturing thoughts is an obedient and powerful tactic of spiritual warfare, taking hold of wrong thinking and wrestling it into a disciplined submission.

The Word of God is the filter through which every thought should pass. We cannot lead others to love the Word of God if we don't esteem, read, memorize, and apply it before them—and that takes discipline.

Scripture is a powerful element of godly discipline. When those old, false mental tapes begin to play, dismiss them with Scripture. When temptation comes or a crisis looms, lean on His truth. We can't use the Word of God unless it is hidden in our hearts. Don't neglect personal time in the Word in order to teach the Word. Personalize Scripture by putting your name in each verse you read. Memorize Scripture, and enlist an accountability partner. When ministry is done from a heart that has digested God's word, it will change lives.

Several years ago, we moved into a house with a huge back yard, which our children immediately proclaimed to be "the perfect spot for a trampoline." Since they had worked so hard helping us move, we rewarded them by buying the trampoline they had wanted for so long.

As we unpacked and assembled it, I unpacked memories from my college years. One of my PE courses included six weeks of instruction on the trampoline. My class couldn't wait to get started! However, before anyone set foot on that trampoline, the professor spent several class periods going over the safety rules. We didn't need rules! How hard could it be? You get on the thing and jump! Not so, according to our teacher. With great persistence, she detailed rule after rule, especially the one about making sure you led your body with your head…or something like that…I really wasn't listening. She persisted, even though it was obvious we were ready for her to be quiet, move out of the way, and let us jump! I guess she thought desperate measures were called for, as she began sharing every injury of every student in every class she had ever taught over the years—injuries that had happened, she said, because the students had been impatient and ignored the rules.

Finally, she ended the class by saying, "Good gymnasts know that where their head goes, the rest of their body will eventually follow." To this day, every time I see a trampoline, those words pop into my mind. And they are just as true when applied to sin.

The Mind Is the Battlefield

In the war with temptation and sin, our greatest battlefield is the mind. We are constantly at war for its control! To live right, we must think right. Proverbs 23:7 says it well: "As he thinks within himself, so he is" (NASB). Everything we do or say originates with a single thought. Filling our minds with truth will fill our lives with truth. Isaiah declares, "You will keep in perfect peace all who trust in you, whose thoughts are fixed on you" (Isaiah 26:3). In this verse, "fixed" literally means "loyal or faithful" and refers to the same kind of faithfulness found in marriage. In order to discipline and guard our thoughts, we must make the commitment of being married to the truth of God.

If, however, our minds are not filled with truth, the enemy will pollute them with lies, preparing soil where temptation and sin can flourish. Polluted minds produce polluted lives, but mind pollution can only happen with our permission. I am amazed at how many women in ministry rarely have a fresh word from God or a new truth found in a daily quiet time with Him. God's Word is a powerful purification system for the mind, reprogramming and training our thoughts to line up with His standards. Depositing His Word into the mind results in holy discernment and God-given strength to recognize and turn away from sin. It is the idea of placing a sentry or guard at the entrance of our mind, giving him the authority to determine what does or does not come in. We are quick to give the custody of our mind away to lesser things, to unworthy goals or desires or thoughts, to sin. Understand that if it is going on in your mind, it is reality—and is often the first step toward the edge of a very dangerous cliff.

The story is told of an eagle perched on a block of ice just above Niagara Falls. As the swift current carried the ice and the great eagle closer to the edge of the falls, he ignored the warning cries of other birds and animals. "I have great and powerful wings," he boasted.

"I can fly from my perch at any time. I can handle it." Suddenly the edge of the falls was only a few feet away, the torrent of water carrying the ice over the powerful cascade. The eagle spread his massive wings to mount up, only to discover it was too late. His claws were frozen into the ice.

Sin is like that. When we allow our minds to "perch" on sinful thought patterns, we entertain destruction. Our arrogance blinds us to the ramifications of sinful behavior, and soon we find ourselves on the brink of disaster, wondering how we got there. How many women in ministry are destroyed by a habit that began with one sinful thought? Discipline your mind.

Second Step: Discipline My Mouth

> Don't use your mouth to tell lies; don't ever say things that are not true (Proverbs 4:24 NCV).

Words are power tools that, in the right hands and used correctly, can build and encourage. In the wrong hands and used incorrectly, words can destroy and defeat. Church bulletins are prime examples of the confusion that misused words can cause. Here are a few real and *interesting* examples:

- "This afternoon there will be a meeting in the south and north end of the church. Children will be baptized at both ends."

- "Tuesday at 5 PM there will be an ice-cream social. All the ladies giving milk—please come early."

- "Wednesday, the Ladies' Literary Society will meet. Mrs. Johnson will sing 'Put Me in My Little Bed' accompanied by the pastor."

- "Thursday at 5 PM there will be a meeting of the Little Mothers Club. All those wishing to become Little Mothers will please meet with the minister in the study."

- "This being Easter Sunday, we will ask Mrs. Brown to come forward and lay an egg on the altar."
- "The ladies of the church have cast off clothing of every kind, and they can be seen in the church basement on Friday afternoon."

Unless filtered through discipline and holiness, words can impart false perspectives and untruths. Solomon offers great wisdom concerning the use of words: "The one who guards his mouth preserves his life. The one who opens wide his lips comes to ruin" (Proverbs 13:3 NASB). If we do not learn to use and control our tongue, it will use and control us! While it is true we need to choose our words carefully, it is also true that the tongue reflects the condition of the heart.

I am not a good patient, and I tend to think most medical rules apply to everyone else in my life—but not to me. After all, I am a woman and a Southerland. It doesn't get much tougher than that. I was recently slammed with a high fever and blinding headache that sent me to bed for days, something highly unusual for me. I called my doctor. When he heard my symptoms, he told me to come immediately and he would make room for me in his already overbooked schedule. His urgency was not encouraging.

The minute I walked in, the receptionist waved me back to the patient area, where a nurse promptly escorted me to an examination room, hurriedly recorded my symptoms, took my temperature, glanced briefly at my tongue, and quickly left the room. Minutes later, my doctor and his nurse walked in and stood on the opposite side of the room, smiling at me. At this point, I realized whatever I had was evidently highly contagious and probably fatal. I felt so awful that the latter was most appealing.

"Mary, I am almost certain you have viral meningitis," the doctor said. Seeing the blank look on my face, he explained, "Your abnormally high fever and severe headache are classic symptoms of meningitis, but we need to run some tests to verify my suspicions. By the way, how long have you had the solid white coating on your tongue?" What coating? Why was the color of my tongue important? He continued, "The health of the tongue is a strong indicator of the health of the body."

The same is true when it comes to the words we speak.

> The mouth speaks the things that are in the heart. Good people have good things in their hearts, and so they say good things. But evil people have evil in their hearts, so they say evil things (Matthew 12:34-35 NCV).

We must discipline our mouths.

Third Step: Discipline My Eyes

> Keep your eyes focused on what is right, and look straight ahead to what is good (Proverbs 4:25 NCV).

In order to withstand temptation and deal with sin, we must set our sight on what is right and good. Our focus needs to be purposeful and resolute because outlook determines outcome. Notice that the right way is always "straight ahead." In fact, this verse indicates that what is right and good is directly in front of us, easy to see and easy to follow. If that is true, why do we keep falling into pits? The answer is simple—because we entertain distractions.

As a woman in ministry, I can easily be distracted from what is right and good. We not only need to guard against any distraction from the truth, but we need to reject anything or anyone who will prevent us from setting our eyes on what is right! The psalmist writes, "Turn my eyes away from worthless things; preserve my life according to your word" (Psalm 119:37 NIV). "I will set before my eyes no vile thing" (Psalm 101:3 NIV). In this verse, "vile" means "evil" or "troubling." I wonder how much of our ministries would be eliminated if these two criteria were applied. Sin will either keep us from the truth, or the truth will keep us from sin. Not only do we turn *away* from what is worthless but we turn *to* what is worthy. Anything that is not feeding mental truth is depleting mental truth and originates with Satan himself. If it is not of God, it will numb us to what is of God if we fail to discipline our eyes.

Fourth Step: Discipline My Steps

Be careful what you do, and always do what is right (Proverbs 4:26 NCV).

When Dan and I were first married, I knew almost nothing about football. In fact, I would often ask, "Honey, who has the ball now?" He was so patient, answering every question without bursting into laughter. Dan's favorite team was the Dallas Cowboys, and his favorite player was Emmitt Smith, their star running back.

During one particular game, Emmitt was playing on grass instead of the artificial turf he preferred. The grass was wet, and he wasn't playing his best game, falling down two plays out of three. Frustrated with his performance, he took himself out of the game to change cleats. It didn't help. In fact, it took three cleat changes before he found the ones that gave him the best footing. He then went on to play a phenomenal game.

Obedience puts us on solid ground. God is not asking us for a season of obedience but for a lifestyle of obedience. Will Rogers once said, "Live your life in such a way, that you would not be ashamed to sell your parrot to the town gossip." In Proverbs 3:6-7 Solomon wrote, "Remember the LORD in all you do, and he will give you success. Don't depend on your own wisdom. Respect the LORD and refuse to do wrong" (NCV). Obedience is remembering and choosing God in everything we do, choosing to walk in His steps, following the path He has set for us.

As women in ministry, we are to live like citizens of a future world, guarding each step to make sure it matches the step of God. Not out of fear but out of love. Not because man observes and keeps score, but because God watches and we want to please Him. "Obey God because you are his children. Don't slip back into your old ways of doing evil; you didn't know any better then" (1 Peter 1:14). We cannot come to Christ and continue to respond to the world in the same way! Our behavior will change along with our perspective, our standards, our motives—everything. As Paul says, we became "a new creation; the old has gone, the new has come" (2 Corinthians 5:17 NIV). This holy discipline sounds like an impossible and overwhelming command. It is—outside the power of God.

As I mentioned earlier, Jered, our son, plays football. He loves the sport and has since he was a little boy. Over the years, he has played several positions, but he always ends up playing fullback. College recruiters say he is a "throwback," explaining that he is built like a true fullback, runs like a true fullback, and thinks like a true fullback. Consequently, he rarely fumbles the ball. He explains his success this way: "Most players who carry the ball either make the mistake of trying to create their own route or end up following the wrong guy. I have blockers assigned to me on every play. Their job is to make a path for me. The minute I get the ball, I put my head down, look for my blockers, watch their feet, and follow them—right across the goal line."

God has already been where He wants us to go. All we have to do is look for Him, watch His steps, and follow them—right across the finish line. Discipline your steps, making sure that they match His.

Fifth Step: Discipline My Body

> Do you not know that your body is a temple of the Holy Spirit, who is in you, whom you have received from God? You are not your own; you were bought at a price. Therefore honor God with your body (1 Corinthians 6:19-20 NIV).

It is much easier to give in to sin or yield to temptation when we are physically depleted. Discipline begins in the mind and then travels to the body. I can hear you groaning already, but stay with me! Sin and temptation often find their greatest opportunity to work in the body. I have struggled with diet and exercise from childhood. Part of my struggle is rooted in "fluffy" genes lovingly passed down to me through several generations of "fluffy" relatives. The remainder of my struggle is firmly rooted in the fact that I enjoy eating, hate exercise, and sometimes use food as an emotional outlet.

Born and raised in Texas, I was a young adult and living on my own before I realized that part of God's creation process included green things called vegetables. The motto in our family was, "If it ain't fried, it ain't right." Gravy was a condiment, and potatoes a staple at every meal. No bread? How can you have a meal without bread? Get the picture?

Consequently, over the years, my weight has fluctuated like a championship yo-yo. Satan rejoiced as I deemed myself "worthy" when I lost the weight and "unworthy" when I gained it back. Guilt and shame attached themselves to every bite of food, while the Battle of the Bulge became the War of Worthiness.

Full-time ministry brought new weapons into the fray. Ridiculously crowded schedules and chronic fatigue seemed to be regarded as holy Medals of Honor, so I signed up and quickly learned the unspoken rules of ministry—rest is for the wicked, exhaustion is for the holy, fast food is for the fully devoted, and burnout is the ultimate goal. (At times I can almost hear Satan standing in the wings, laughing at our skewed priorities and lack of discipline, knowing his opening is just around the corner.)

There is simply no way around the truth that discipline of the body is part of a godly life. We cannot give our hearts to God but keep our bodies for ourselves. To do so is sin. It's time for a new plan and a new way of thinking when it comes to disciplining the body.

1. Eliminate Diets

Replace all "diets" with a "healthy eating plan." Fad diets are a quick fix and rarely work long-term. A healthy eating plan requires a change in lifestyle and is not only a matter of how much we weigh, but a matter of what we eat as well. Many thin people follow diets that are just as ungodly as the diets of overweight people. I have begun asking myself, *Is this good for me?* instead of, *Is this fattening?* A healthy eating plan honors God.

2. Get Moving

A friend once told me that her favorite exercise was opening and closing the refrigerator door. Hmm…not good! Set realistic goals in the area of exercise. Start with 20 minutes a day, three times a week. Gradually increase the time spent exercising. Choose an activity with a dual purpose. For example, while you are walking you can pray. Walking can be a healthy way of dealing with anger, venting frustration to God instead of others. A walk can also serve as a "mini-retreat" during a chaotic day. Ask God to change your perspective on exercise—then take the first step. He will meet you there.

3. Learn to Rest

Rest is not an option if we are to function at our best. We sometimes try to feed emotional needs by refusing to rest. After all, the world will surely fall apart without our input—or will it? Perhaps we stay busy because we're afraid to face our past or even the future. Guilt keeps us moving, trying to prove our worth.

For most of my adult life, I have wrongly equated being busy with being productive. I am guilty as charged when it comes to living each day in overdrive. My Day-Timer has, at times, been my Bible. The result has always, always been exhaustion, burnout, and watered-down ministry. Everything looked great on the outside, but God and I both knew that the façade I had so carefully erected was nothing more than a meaningless monument to self. The house built upon the sand seemed like very familiar digs. And I was not alone.

Ministry is filled with both men and women who use ministry as a platform for self-promotion. We are masters of rationalizing our way to man's approval. I am convinced that when we are willing to surrender our lives to the tyranny of the urgent, the enemy will keep 'em coming—people who need you immediately, those who clamor

> Jesus…modeled the truth that it is in Sabbath moments we will find Him most precious and hear His voice more clearly.

for your attention above your family and personal relationship with God, or the person who can talk to no one but you. The list goes on. What ego strokes they bring—and what futility.

Through the years, God has grabbed my attention with an illness that drove me to bed or a crisis that drove me to my knees. He is a persistent Father who understands the value of rest. Jesus even modeled the truth that it is in Sabbath moments we will find Him most precious and hear His voice more clearly. After all, He was in charge of the creation process, which included the need for rest. Did God *need* to rest? Obviously not, but by creating a day of rest, He drove home the fact that our bodies were created in such a way that rest is not an option. Make no mistake, we will rest—one way or another. The psalmist writes, "He gives me rest in green pastures" (Psalm 23:2 ICB). I know from my own experience that the word "make" holds worlds of possibilities from God's hand. Learning to rest demands an understanding of several basic truths.

Rest is sacred. Sometimes the most spiritual thing we can do is sleep. The human body is programmed for a certain amount of rest. We can cheat it short-term—not long-term! Rest affects the efficiency rating of this frail body in which we dwell.

Rest is replenishing. While we rest, the Father repairs and restores. We run on "batteries" that must be recharged daily. When I am tired, it is much harder for me to handle stress—and I know you will agree with me when I say ministry can be stressful.

Rest reduces stress. Doctors say that stress can be good or bad, but either way, stress takes its toll. Elijah is a great example of good stress gone bad! One day he was the conquering hero, the next day we find him sitting under a juniper tree begging God to let him die! The poor man was exhausted. It was stress produced by victory, but stress nonetheless.

Rest eliminates fatigue. Fatigue is not a spiritual gift, but in ministry we proudly wear dark-circled eyes as badges of honor and sacrificial service. The enemy loves it! If he can keep us exhausted, we are little threat to him.

We must not only learn to rest but learn *when* we need to rest as well! I have discovered an irritating truth with no escape clause—we need to rest most when we have the least amount of time to rest. I hate the fact that God calls me from my vicious cycle of religious activity into His presence. After all, I spent a lot of time getting all of those irons into the fire I built with my own ideas and plans. However, every time I obey His call to "come apart," He transforms ineffective religious activity into powerful, life-transforming ministry—true ministry. We need to stop—be still—and rest.

4. Learn to Fast

Consistent fasting produces both physical and spiritual discipline and control. Try fasting one meal this week. Next week, fast two meals on the same day, and during the third week, fast the entire day. Be sure to drink water and juices, and take the time you would normally spend eating to pray and read the Bible. Fasting leads to physical and spiritual cleansing as it paves the way for godly discipline.

As women in ministry, we know and teach the truth that our bodies house the Holy Spirit. In what condition is your dwelling place for God? Is He pleased with His temple? A lack of physical discipline is a foothold for the enemy, an unlocked door through which disobedience and failure ride on the wings of Satan's best schemes. It is time for us to embrace and apply physical discipline as a gift and commandment from God.

Sixth Step: Discipline My Time

> Conduct yourselves wisely toward outsiders, making the most of the time (Colossians 4:5 NRSV).

Time management is a dreaded and often ignored spiritual discipline. We choose where to invest our time, carefully planning everything from committee meetings and church activities to lunch appointments and choir practice—but we fail to schedule the most important activity of all, spending time with God. Being wrapped up in God's work can easily become a shabby substitute for being wrapped up in Him. Discipline carves out time to sit at His feet.

Sin thrives in an out-of-control life, a life without godly discipline. Temptation happily dances across overcrowded schedules. Our minutes, hours, and days are precious commodities, gifts from God that can be unwrapped only once. We can become so busy meeting the needs of others that we destroy ourselves in the process.

I cannot tell you how many women I know who have given themselves away for so long that there's nothing left to give. Today, there are men selling insurance and women manning a corporate desk because they allowed ministry to consume them and had to walk away in order to survive. Marriages fail, children rebel, and ministry fails because flawed priorities dictate wrong living.

Let me be very clear on this point. Authentic ministry empowers and energizes the minister. I often hear ministers joke, "Why, I'd rather burn out than rust out!" The problem with that statement is that either way—they are out! The absence of godly discipline is too often the culprit behind ministry dropouts.

After being in ministry for many years, I am firmly convinced that the role of women in ministry is unique. From the beginning of time, God has used women to lead His people, build His church, and accomplish His plan. He has neither changed His mind nor altered His plan for women in ministry today, but in an effort to prove ourselves, our worth, and our calling, we rush headlong through pointless days. I often hear the flawed thinking, "Mary, it's true I'm very busy, but I'm busy doing good things." Those words were the cry of my heart just before I crashed and burned, landing in a pit of clinical depression—a monument to my insecurity.

A Question of Investment

From the bottom of that pit, it was easy to see just how skewed my perspective of time really was. I had poured years into making my plan successful, only to discover that God gives resources to and empowers His plan alone. It was painfully obvious I needed an attitude adjustment, an eternal perspective kindled by godly discipline. I needed to understand my time was not really mine but a treasure on loan to me from God. He wanted me to understand He was calling me to work *from* His love and acceptance—not *toward* it! Every plan, priority, and goal must be held against the backdrop of eternity because it is from that backdrop that our priorities are validated, our calling confirmed, and our time best invested.

A young and successful executive was traveling down a neighborhood street, going a bit too fast in his new Jaguar. He was watching for kids darting out from between parked cars and slowed down when he thought he saw something. As his car passed, no children appeared. Instead, a brick smashed into the Jag's side door! He slammed on the brakes and backed up to the spot where the brick had been thrown. Angrily, he jumped out, grabbed the nearest kid, and pushed him up against a parked car, shouting, "Just what the heck are you doing? That's a new car, and that brick you threw is going to cost a lot of money. Why did you do it?" The young boy was apologetic. "Please, mister...please, I'm sorry but I didn't know what else to do," he pleaded. "I threw the brick because no one else would stop."

With tears dripping down his face and off his chin, the boy pointed to a spot just beyond another car. "It's my brother. He rolled off the curb and fell out of his wheelchair, and I can't lift him up." Now sobbing, the boy asked the stunned executive, "Would you please help me get him back into his wheelchair? He's hurt, and he's too heavy for me."

Moved beyond words, the driver tried to swallow the rapidly swelling lump in his throat. He hurriedly lifted the handicapped boy back into the wheelchair, then took out a linen handkerchief and dabbed at the fresh scrapes and cuts. A quick look told him everything was going to be okay. "Thank you, and God bless you," the grateful child told the stranger. Too shook up for words, the man watched the boy push his wheelchair-bound brother down the sidewalk toward their home.

It was a long, slow walk back to his Jaguar. The damage was very noticeable, but the man never bothered to repair the door. He kept the dent there to remind him of this message: "Don't go through life so fast that someone has to throw a brick at you to get your attention!" God whispers in our souls and speaks to our hearts. Sometimes when we are busy and think we don't have time to listen, He throws a brick at us.

Let's face it. If we don't set priorities for life and for ministry, others will. Time thieves will steal the hours and days as we allow them to impose their plans and demands on us. While it is true that different women have different priorities in different seasons of ministry, it is also true that one priority remains steadfast: "Seek first the kingdom of God" (Matthew 6:33 NKJV). Once that priority is firmly established, the rest of life and ministry will simply fall into place.

Godly priorities embrace God's plan. I am convinced that much of our frustration in ministry comes from doing things we were never intended to do. We create the plan as we go instead of resting in the plan He has for us. Discipline guides each step and establishes a basis for obedience and success in ministry.

I am by no means an expert in the area of discipline, but I do want to share with you some simple ideas that work for me.

Prepare. Just as we budget our money, we must budget our time. Every day, we are presented with 24 hours, and every day we must choose to either spend those hours or invest them. Every Sunday afternoon, I do two things—write a weekly column and plan the week ahead. I assign tasks to each day and prioritize those tasks in order of importance. That's the easy part. The hard part is sticking to the plan, but getting a head start offers a greater chance for success. Schedule one day a week to plan. The preparation will pay off.

Eliminate. Once a month, have a family "spring cleaning." Go out to dinner, and together, eliminate anything that is hurting your family. Make a purposeful plan for adding only those activities that will strengthen each member of your family. I am convinced the reason many children of ministers grow up to resent the church is because they feel it has robbed them of their parents.

Prioritize. Learn to leave the "lesser" things undone. This lesson is especially hard for me because I actually believe I can do it all! The key to godly discipline and right priorities is learning what my "all" is, and doing all of that! Admittedly, my trusty "Superwoman" cape is never far away, and it is a constant battle for me to ignore the presence of that cape, choosing rather to embrace and employ God's priorities—not mine. But it is definitely a battle worth fighting. Families, marriage, ministries, and souls are on the line.

A right perspective is the direct result of godly discipline. In order to have right priorities, we must have right perspectives. Godly discipline brings a holy scrutiny to priorities and perspectives: *Does it really matter? Is it eternal? Will it impact lives for God?*

Delegate. Include every family member in the work, and include every family member in the play. The concept of "team" is essential to every successful family. A chore is not just a random assignment. It says, "You are an important part of this team—this family. We need you."

Simplify. Give up on perfection. It is meant for heaven…not earth! I love the Amish saying, "The further we get from simple things, the further we get from God." Jesus was born in sparse simplicity, a manger instead of a mansion. His teachings were simple enough for a child to understand. Simple but stunning truth is His message. We often overlook profound simplicity in search of hollow complexity, foolishly thinking that bigger is always better. When it comes to investing time, we need to employ simple godly discipline.

Yield. When our children were small, I did not travel and speak as often as I do now. My greatest mission field is my home, my marriage, and my children—easy words to write, but hard words to live.

It does not matter how much we do or how successful we are in ministry. If home and family are left with only the scraps of our time, energy, and emotions, we are walking in sin and disobedience.

The Challenges Are Worth It

One of the greatest challenges in my life is to achieve and maintain a disciplined balance. I am not certain why balance is so hard to achieve, but one reason stands out from the rest—self. If "self" were a coin, one side of that coin would be pride. Earning the favor of God, proving my worth, and longing for success feed that pride. The opposite side of the coin is insecurity. Believing the lies of the enemy, measuring my worth by what I do instead of whose I am, and longing for man's applause and earth's acclaim can be counted on to fuel the tormenting fires of insecurity.

Both pride and insecurity are sin. Both are a preoccupation with self. Godly discipline draws attention to God and away from self, to His work and away from human effort, leaving the glory where it belongs—at His feet alone.

The most effective ministry comes from a disciplined life. Discipline builds upon discipline, each success encouraging another. Make the commitment to cultivate the disciplines of a godly woman, then pick a corner of your life and begin. Discipline does not come naturally or easily. We will surely fail, but we can always begin again. Join me today in a new commitment to choosing to seek, apply, and relish godly discipline.

> Though no one can go back
> and make a brand-new start, my friend,
> Quite anyone can start from new
> and make a brand-new end.
>
> AUTHOR UNKNOWN

> A man may be consecrated, dedicated and devoted
> but of little value if undisciplined.
>
> HUDSON TAYLOR

On a personal note, I honestly did not want to write this chapter and tried unsuccessfully to talk the Father out of my doing so. You see, while I hate the very word "discipline," most people would describe me as a disciplined woman. If they only knew!

Discipline is a constant battle for me—in every area of life. Just when I have one area mastered (or so I think), another one falls apart! I want to be a champion for God, but I have to admit that I am often a miserable failure when it comes to discipline. My only hope is God and His power at work in me. The principles of holy discipline will ensure the life of a champion and allow us to experience the power of God in ministry.

How to Relish Godly Discipline

Key verse: "Trust in the Lord with all your heart and lean not on your own understanding; in all your ways acknowledge him, and he will make your paths straight" (Proverbs 3:5-6 NIV).

Key truths: I think I'm safe in saying we all want to be successful in ministry, but we can easily become confused, even lost and unsure about which way to go. A bigger church calls to offer you a new position. Your marriage is slowly eroding before your eyes. Your best friend has become your worst enemy. Your children seem to have no desire for God, money is always tight, and stress is eating your lunch.

We are no different than the people to whom we minister. Same problems—same dreams—same fears—same hopes. Yet hardly a day goes by that I don't hear of someone whose life and ministry is in trouble because of a moral failure, exhaustion, burnout, or divorce—in other words, a lack of discipline. Why? We don't trust God. What does trust have to do with discipline? Everything!

Trust is the cornerstone of discipline. The word "trust" in Proverbs 3:5 literally means, "to lie helpless, face down." It is the picture of a servant who is waiting for his master's command or a soldier yielding himself to a conquering general. Trusting God requires total abandonment to Him. It means coming to Him with no hidden agenda, with one word in our hearts: "Whatever! Whatever you want me to do, Lord, I will do. Whatever you want me to say, I will say. Whatever you want me to think, I will think. Whatever path you have for me is the path I will walk."

At times, I have problems trusting God—and I suspect you do as well. It is amazing to me I would ever doubt Him after all He has done in my life. I have examined the uncertainty that nips at my heels and threatens to drown me in a sea of fear and have come to one conclusion. A lack of trust and a lack of discipline go hand-in-hand, because we don't know God intimately. It is hard to trust and fully surrender to someone we don't know very well. Intimacy breeds trust, and trust encourages discipline.

Application steps:

- Read Proverbs 3:1-4. This passage offers four disciplines that encourage trust in God. List them below.

  1. _____

  2. _____

  3. _____

  4. _____

True or false: Discipline is basic to the growth of every believer. Explain your answer.

_____

_____

- Choose to apply new godly habits in each of the following areas. List each habit.

  Mind: _____

  Mouth: _____

  Eyes: _____

  Steps: _____

  Body: _____

  Time: _____

- Yield to the Holy Spirit and allow Him to work in your life.

- Decide now to reject anyone or anything that undermines your trust in God.

Memory verse: "The fear of the Lord is the beginning of knowledge, but fools despise wisdom and discipline" (Proverbs 1:7 NIV).

Reflection point: *Godly discipline allows us to rest within the framework of God's sovereignty.*

Record any thoughts or fresh insights concerning the above statement:

_____

_____

_____

Power verses:

Happy are those whom you discipline, LORD, and those whom you teach from your law (Psalm 94:12).

Those whom I love I rebuke and discipline. So be earnest, and repent (Revelation 3:19 NIV).

Anyone who loves learning accepts correction, but a person who hates being corrected is stupid (Proverbs 12:1 NCV).

One new truth:

_____

_____

D	Desperate
I	I
S	Stood
C	Captured
I	In
P	Pride
L	Love
I	Irresistible
N	Now
E	Embraced

My Journey
A Life Story by Tania Haber

Tania Haber *serves as senior pastor at Westwood Lutheran Church in St. Louis Park, Minnesota (a suburb of Minneapolis). Her husband, Bob Wertz, is also a senior pastor...in another congregation...so they cherish family vacation time together! They have two daughters: Ali, 15; and Sophie, 12. In her "free time," Tania is a Suzuki violin parent for both daughters and loves to sail on Lake Superior.*

The LORD will watch over your coming and going both now and forevermore (Psalm 121:8 NIV).

Having just celebrated 20 years as a parish pastor, I think of this comforting promise daily—that no matter the challenges, the drudgery, or the joys the day will hold, God is with us.

From childhood, I dreamed of marrying a pastor and serving the church, but my heart was struggling with how to live out this call of God on my life. I entered college two years after the Lutheran Church began ordaining women. But living in South Dakota, I had yet to see or hear an ordained woman—until one morning when a young woman climbed into the pulpit of my college chapel. She was not only the guest preacher but a pastor as well. My heart raced with excitement, and my eyes were opened. That morning I saw and heard what I knew God had been calling me to for many years. For the fifth time, I changed my major, this time to religion. After graduation, I worked in campus ministry for two years, where my call was affirmed. I headed to seminary and continued preparing for ministry.

Having served four congregations now (two as an associate pastor, and two as the senior pastor), I can honestly say I can't imagine doing anything else! I remain passionate about what I'm doing and grateful for the opportunity to serve in this way.

Has the journey been rough because I'm a woman? No. I've been fortunate to serve congregations with colleagues and parishioners who wholeheartedly accepted and supported me as a pastor, a wife, and a mother. My husband, who is a senior pastor in another congregation, and our two daughters, who have already hit the ages where they should be embarrassed by the fact that both parents are clergy, have been my biggest cheerleaders.

I guess you could say that I broke the "glass ceiling" by being the first woman senior pastor in our synod. I have never pushed the issue of being a woman pastor because I am simply one more person seeking to live out the calling of God in my heart.

This journey can be lonely, but I believe I share that feeling with my male colleagues. The church is at a crossroads today, especially for those of us serving in mainline denominations. Our job is not as clear as it may have been a few decades back. It is a daily struggle to tell the "old, old story" in new, creative, and powerful ways, especially for those of us in hundred-year-old congregations full of history and tradition.

Has the journey been rough? Yes, but only because I'm a follower of Christ. Just like you, male or female, all of us who live under the cross face a life of tension with the world, a life of challenges, letdowns, doubts, and pain. The place where the cross and the world intersect is not an easy one, but as Rick Warren once said, "If you can think of anything more important or more fulfilling to do with your life than live this adventure with Jesus Christ—then do it." As for me, I can't imagine anything better!

Has the journey been joyful? Almost always! I have always served in congregations with both male and female clergy and have experienced the delights of working on a team with the unique gifts and perspectives of both men and women. Mothers in my congregation tell me their five-year-old daughters "play pastor" and baptize their dolls. Several teenage girls are considering attending seminary. How exciting to see these young followers of Christ for whom the doors are now open to live out the call of God in their hearts.

If you are wrestling with where God might be calling you, I am proof God's call may lead to a place you can't even imagine right now. Follow the yearning God has placed in your heart. Walk through the doors that are perhaps barely open, and let God's Spirit blow you through!

🐾 🐾 🐾

Habit 4:

Pursue God's Vision

On the first day of school, a professor challenged each member of his class to meet someone new. As one young man stood to begin his search, a gentle hand touched his shoulder. Turning, he found a wrinkled little old lady with dancing eyes and a dazzling smile. "Hi! My name is Rose," she said. "I'm eighty-seven years old." The student laughed as she grabbed him in a fierce hug. "Why are you in college at such a young, innocent age?" he asked. Rose jokingly replied, "I'm here to meet a rich husband, get married, and have a couple of kids." "No, seriously," the young man persisted, curious about what may have motivated her to take on this challenge at her age. "I always dreamed of having a college education, and now I'm getting one!" she said.

After class, they walked to the student-union building and shared a chocolate milkshake. They became instant friends and every day for the next three months would leave class together, talking nonstop. Over the course of the year, Rose became a campus icon, easily making friends wherever she went. She loved to dress up and delighted in the attention from other students. In short, Rose was living it up!

At the end of the semester, the students invited Rose to speak at their annual banquet. As she began to deliver her prepared speech, Rose accidentally dropped her three-by-five cards on the floor. Frustrated and a little embarrassed, she leaned into the microphone and simply said, "I'm sorry I'm so jittery. I gave up beer for Lent, and this whiskey is killing me! I'll never get my speech back in order so let me just tell you what I know."

As everyone laughed, she cleared her throat and began. "You've got to have a dream. When you lose your dreams, you die. There are so many people walking around who are dead and don't even know it! There is a huge difference between growing older and growing up. Anybody can grow older. That doesn't take any talent or ability. The idea is to grow up by always finding the opportunity in change. Have no regrets. The elderly usually don't have regrets about what we did, but about what we didn't do. The only people who fear death are those with regrets." Rose concluded her speech by courageously singing "The Rose," challenging the students to study the lyrics and live them out in their daily lives.

At the year's end, Rose finished the college degree she had begun many years ago. One week after graduation, she died peacefully in her sleep. More than 2000 college students attended her funeral, paying tribute to the wonderful woman who had taught by example that it's never too late to be all you can possibly be. It's never too late to dream.[*]

---

[*] Adapted from an Internet source. Author unknown.

Comfort vs. Change

Powerful ministry is the natural result of God's vision fed by God's power at work in God's people who dare to dream. If we want to experience the power of God in ministry, we have to be willing to dream new dreams and pursue new visions. "In the last days, God says, 'I will pour out my Spirit on all people. Your sons and daughters will prophesy, your young men will see visions, your old men will dream dreams'" (Acts 2:17 NIV). Dreams are costly. Vision demands sacrifice and a willingness to change. Change is hard—but it's essential for the growth and maturity of any living thing.

The body of Christ is alive, but many parts of it are not healthy because they refuse to change and, in doing so, refuse to grow. Any living thing that does not grow and change will eventually die. I will be quick to admit it is much easier to stay in the harbor of comfort than it is to make your way through the rough waters of change, but I also know those rough waters are easier to navigate if you are not in the rocking boat alone. My husband and I have navigated a treacherous passage of transition and lived to tell about it. Climb into the boat as I share our story.

> "The only person who really likes change is a wet baby." Every transition, every change, was incredibly intense and personal and had built-in opposition.

Dan thought he would always work with youth, but I knew he would one day pastor a church. I was right. In the fall of 1989, God called Dan to be the pastor of Flamingo Road Church in Ft. Lauderdale, Florida. This traditional church of 300 was at a crossroads and had just experienced its second stretch in three years of being without a pastor or staff. The church hired Dan, a worship leader and a youth pastor—and began what became the ride of a lifetime!

Flamingo Road experienced solid growth over the next several months. By the spring of 1990, we were well on our way to becoming a large traditional church. Then we made a heartbreaking discovery: We were not reaching lost people. Our growth was 90 percent transfers from other churches and only 10 percent people won to Christ.

That discovery began a new journey of discovering how to do church for the unchurched. We diligently studied other churches with the same mission, and after a year of studying, seeking, and praying, we began to make the change. God blessed us in amazing ways as we made nine specific transitions:

- *Approach:* from program-driven to purpose-driven
- *Target:* from reaching "fellow Baptists" to reaching the unchurched
- *Worship style:* from traditional to contemporary
- *Leadership:* from a committee/deacon-led church to a staff-led church
- *Pastors:* from a senior-pastor model to a team approach
- *Ministry:* from staff doing the entire ministry, to staff being equippers and lay ministers doing the ministry
- *Strategy:* from no systematic plan for reaching the lost or developing new believers to a life-cycle process driven by small groups
- *Small groups:* from a traditional Sunday-school model to a relationship-centered small-group model
- *Schedule:* from one worship service to five worship services each weekend

Flamingo Road grew to a church of 2300 in attendance by 2002. We started 23 mission churches that now total another 5000 in worship attendance. Today, 70 percent of those who join are unchurched before they come. God has done a "new thing." As my husband says, though, "The only person who really likes change is a wet baby." Every transition, every change, was incredibly intense and personal and had built-in opposition. In the midst of all the changes, I broke. In fact, the transition process of Flamingo Road was one of the main reasons for my two-year struggle with clinical depression. I did not know how to handle the blatant opposition, the emotional pain, or the personal attacks.

Part of my time in that dark pit of depression was spent, not only learning how to survive transition, but coming to the place of actually thriving on transition and change. It is those lessons I want to share with you.

Lesson One: Take Control of Your Emotions

> My child, listen to me and do as I say, and you will have a long, good life. I will teach you wisdom's ways and lead you in straight paths. If you live a life guided by wisdom, you won't limp or stumble as you run. Carry out my instructions; don't forsake them. Guard them, for they will lead you to a fulfilled life (Proverbs 4:10-13).

Transition must be fueled by spiritual wisdom, not human emotion. Changing a method of worship and style of music in worship is a personal issue. Intense emotions will inevitably surface. Emotions are often difficult to manage, especially negative emotions. Women in ministry are no exception to this struggle. In fact, I suspect we are prime candidates for frequent emotional skirmishes.

You have probably discovered you simply can't trust your emotions, because they are unreliable, misleading, and will constantly betray you. A church member verbally blasts you, and rage consumes your spirit. Your ministry is in decline, and depression slithers into your heart. Caught in the comparison trap, you find yourself avoiding those who have bigger, more influential ministries. Anger is a constant companion, finances are tight, and rest is a distant memory. A sense of bone-deep weariness saturates your soul as your own heart ridicules the sincerity with which you serve. *You might as well give up. It's no use. Just quit!* the enemy taunts.

At times, ministry may seem like the perfect setting for negative emotions to take hold of and destroy a life. But ministry is also the perfect setting for emotional control to shine. Control puts emotions in their God-shaped place, discarding negative emotions as the spiritual leeches they are, while safeguarding and reinforcing positive emotions. I am amazed at the number of women in ministry who base eternal decisions on feelings—seeking confirmation and even direction from emotional responses. I almost missed one of the highest plans for my life because it didn't *feel* right.

Dan was a youth pastor at Sheridan Hills Baptist, a dynamic church in Hollywood, Florida, where Bill Billingsley, one of the greatest men I have ever known, was senior pastor. He and his amazing wife, Betty Jean, had an enormous impact on me personally, and on the ministry of speaking and writing to which God has now called me. It was in the midst of my God-ordained transformation at Sheridan Hills and the youth program's greatest growth that Dan dropped the bomb—he felt God calling him back to Southwestern Seminary in Fort Worth, Texas. Well, I felt God calling him to stay put!

I loved Sheridan Hills! It was home! Going back to seminary meant I would have to go back to teaching elementary school. Teaching wasn't the problem, but placing Jered in day care was. We had waited so long for this chosen baby, and the thought of relegating his care to strangers broke my heart. How could this possibly be God's plan when it *felt* so wrong?

My favorite worship time at Sheridan Hills was the Wednesday-night service—for two reasons. I enjoyed the contemporary worship and in-depth Bible teaching. I also treasured the fact that, each week, while Dan was in meetings and Jered was in the nursery, I could slip into the empty, darkened auditorium for an hour of solitude. However, the Wednesday night after Dan shared the numbing probability of our return to seminary, my usually refreshing solitude dissolved into a tantrum of crying, praying, and pleading with God to let us stay.

When a hand gently patted my shoulder, I looked up into the tear-filled eyes of my pastor. "I have something to tell you," he said. Pastor Billingsley was not only a spiritual mentor in my life, but a loving father figure as well. Expecting a word of wisdom or encouragement, I was shattered by his words: "I have cancer." Speechless, we sat in pain-filled silence, weeping; each flailing in our own sea of emotions and questions. Bill Billingsley then spoke the words that have guided my steps from the moment he spoke them forth. "Mary, just remember that God's will penalizes no one."

I immediately knew I had a choice to make. I could defiantly hold on to my emotional comfort, or submit to God's will. Going back to seminary proved to be a spiritual marker for our family. At first, I cried every day and seethed in anger each night. I couldn't blame God, so I blamed Dan! I missed being home with Jered, even though he loved the seminary day care and Miss Nancy, his incredibly gifted and caring teacher. I complained about others raising my son, even though Dan picked him up after lunch each day and kept him every afternoon. I resented having to work, even though my teaching assignment was at one of the best elementary schools in Fort Worth and my principal was a precious Christian man.

Gradually, God broke my hardened heart as I realized Jered was flourishing in day care as he made wonderful friends, learned how to adjust to changes, and enjoyed priceless time with his dad. Teaching school became a passion and, in many ways, prepared me for the calling I now live. Had my emotions ruled, I would have missed God's best for my life.

Looking back, I now see I gave negative emotions free reign. The result was wasted emotional energy, health problems, spiritual disobedience, and mental exhaustion. Do not walk that path, my friend. Instead, right now, commit to emotional integrity and discipline. God will surely empower that commitment.

Emotions are a gift from God. While emotions themselves are not sin, the place we give them can be. Since God created us with the capacity for strong emotions, we can rest assured He has a plan for managing them. It is a step-by-step plan that begins with our commitment to being honest and transparent about every emotion, especially the negative ones.

1. Identify the Source of Negative Emotions

Negative emotions are nourished in many ways—by daily challenges, a painful past, hurt or rejection, an undisciplined thought life, or Satan himself. Some people qualify as "carriers" because they not only transmit negative emotions but constantly use others as their personal dumping ground. In managing negative emotions, it is imperative we identify their source and eliminate it.

2. Label Negative Emotions Correctly

Women in ministry are masters at mislabeling emotions because we fear that exposing our true emotions will affect the way others see us. It is time for us to take off and burn the emotional masks we wear. Healing and restoration begin at the point of emotional integrity! I believe that vision demands total abandonment of self to God and blatant emotional transparency before man. Oh, yes—and vision changes everything in its path!

With each change at Flamingo Road, people we considered friends left the church in a storm of brutal criticism. I had never experienced such pain and rejection. I knew I wasn't supposed to take it personally, but it seemed very personal. I labeled my emotional response as "hurt," but God called it "hatred"—and when I refused His command to deal with that hatred, He called it "murder." It was not until I was willing to acknowledge the depth of my pain, calling it what it really was, that I began to experience peace and healing. It is impossible to deal with negative emotions until we face them with raw transparency, identify their source and surrender each one to God's healing touch.

3. Learn to Manage Emotions

It is not enough to acknowledge the presence of negative emotions or even understand why they exist. We must take action. If we don't, negative emotions will take control—a dangerous proposition for women in ministry. We must not only be able to manage negative emotions in our own lives, we must be able to react correctly to negative emotions produced by the sometimes abrasive behavior of those to whom we minister. And seekers—those who are interested in Christ—watch carefully, curious to see what happens when the pressure is on.

So many women in ministry are imprisoned by feelings of inferiority. And the results are always disastrous. Constructive criticism is perceived as an emotional attack. Jealousy burgeons as others receive the accolades we desperately crave. Decisions are made and a course of ministry is determined so fragile egos can be fed, excluding God's plan and purpose. Comparison reigns as a false idol in the attempt to validate worth and success. Inferiority crosses over to pride, and sin reigns.

Every woman in ministry knows that emotions can be like runaway horses. You are trampled by some committee with a hidden agenda, kicked in the gut by a fellow staff member, thrown by the lies of a church member, or crushed by a lack of integrity and character in those in authority over you. Emotions can easily stampede out of control and into sin.

On the other hand, we can put negative emotions to work in our lives. The success of emotional integrity lies in the one who holds the reins. We must constantly choose to surrender every emotion to the supernatural control of God because when we do, the Holy Spirit empowers that choice, produces control, and transforms emotional bondage into emotional freedom. Learning to control anger is a crucial life lesson and, as women in ministry, one we need to master.

The people around us want to see what happens when life pushes our buttons or squeezes our emotions. While God created us with the capacity for emotions, it is our responsibility to control them instead of allowing them to control us.

When Jesus saw money changers desecrating the temple of God, He was furious! Yet He modeled the right way to harness emotions and use them for good. I have heard many Bible teachers and preachers attempt to soften the emotional response of Jesus, but the truth is, He was irate! I can almost see His face shrouded in plain old fury as He contemplated His options. If I had been in His place, those wicked men would have been toast, I can tell you! But before Jesus faced the intruders, He stepped aside to braid a whip—not because He had completed "Whip Braiding 101," but because, I believe, He was taking the time to harness His emotions. He then used that harnessed anger to drive the money changers out of the temple, correcting a wrong. We choose where to invest every ounce of emotional energy we possess. Like Jesus, we must learn to invest wisely in order to reap the benefits of healthy emotions, harnessed and trained by godly discipline.

Emotional bankruptcy is too often responsible for women leaving ministry, churches faltering, and sure callings doubted. When we value programs over people, success over obedience, or comfort over character, the result is a life without balance and a ministry without purpose. We must intentionally monitor emotional withdrawals and the impact they will have on the ministry to which God has called us.

Ministry provides the opportunity for countless withdrawals from our emotional "bank account"—ones that are good, right, and ordained by God. I will never forget the night we found a broken and defeated young pastor standing at our front door. With tears streaming down his face, John told us his wife was having an affair and wanted a divorce. Certain his ministry was doomed, this precious and gifted servant poured out his pain and defeat. For months, Dan and I ministered to this young man, loving him, encouraging him, making him part of our family while he tried desperately to save his marriage.

When it became clear his wife was determined to leave him, we repeatedly assured John that God would once again use him for kingdom work. Today, that once broken young man is married to a beautiful, godly woman who adores him, and together, they have two incredible children. The church he now pastors is exploding in growth, changing lives, and impacting the world for Jesus Christ! The time and energy we poured into John was a worthy emotional investment, to say the least, and one of our greatest blessings in ministry.

However, some emotional "withdrawals" are not good, right, healthy, or God-ordained! Ministry is jam-packed with lifeless places in which to invest emotional energy. There are those who look to us, as women in ministry, to be their faithful savior or their always-available crisis manager. Well, that job belongs to God alone!

We all know about bounced checks. For the life of me, I cannot figure out why banks don't adopt my obviously superior philosophy about checking accounts. It goes something like this: "As long as there are checks, there is money." Sadly, my current bank is rather narrow-minded in this area, so the reality is that our checks will bounce when our bank account is overdrawn and out of balance. The same is true in ministry.

We constantly need to check our emotional balance, guarding the emotional withdrawals we allow and diligently making consistent emotional deposits. Prayer, solitude, Bible study, friendships, service, accountability, and a guarded thought life are just a few of the deposits that can make the difference between emotional health and emotional bankruptcy. Paul says it well:

> God has made us what we are. In Christ Jesus, God made us to do good works, which God planned in advance for us to live our lives doing (Ephesians 2:10 NCV).

In other words, we need to do what God has called us to do—period. We must pursue His vision—not ours.

Emotional imbalance occurs when we operate in our own strength, doing our "own thing" instead of wholly depending upon God and living in the parameters of His will. When we abandon all that we are to His strength, purpose, and power, the Father deposits everything we need to pursue the vision to which He has called us.

Lesson Two: Recruit a Support Team

> The way of the righteous is like the first gleam of dawn, which shines ever brighter until the full light of day. But the way of the wicked is like complete darkness. Those who follow it have no idea what they are stumbling over (Proverbs 4:18-19).

Ministry can be a very lonely place—but it doesn't have to be. Do not buy the lie that women in ministry cannot have friends in the church. A support team is essential during times of transition, because a shared load is a lighter load. Friends offer accountability, strength, encouragement, and a fresh perspective. I love the promise of Ecclesiastes 4:12: "An enemy might defeat one person, but two people together can defend themselves. A rope that has three parts wrapped together is hard to break" (ICB). We were created to need each other.

During one of the most difficult stretches of transition at Flamingo Road, I began a personal campaign for Dan to become a travel agent…until I received a phone call from a woman of great wisdom, a faithful member of the church. Her voice was filled with warmth and encouragement. "Mary, Jim and I would love for you and Dan to come for dinner tonight. We have already arranged for a babysitter to keep Jered and Danna. What do you say?" Let's see, that meant no cooking, no cleaning, no wrestling with small children, and eating delicious food served on a plate instead fake food wrapped in paper. Tough decision! "We would love to come, Geri!" I responded.

The meal was delicious, the evening relaxing and fun! Jim seemed determined to share every funny story he knew. We laughed until we cried. This precious couple then asked if they could pray for us. "We want you both to know we pray for you every day," they said. "We love you and are completely behind you. So, when things get rough, just remember we are here for you, on our knees." These two prayer warriors proceeded to pray for us, our children, the church, every need, and every concern. We left, replenished and restored. It was an invaluable reprieve from the battle and a powerful reminder of how important it is to have a support team. Jesus did.

I have often wondered why Jesus bothered with the 12 disciples. I believe one reason is that Jesus, come to Earth as man, needed a support team around Him to do what God had called Him to do. It was not because Jesus lacked the power to accomplish the task His Father had given Him; it was because He needed friends. If Jesus needed a support team, we certainly do.

Lesson Three: Avoid the Whiners

> Do not do as the wicked do or follow the path of evil-doers. Avoid their haunts. Turn away and go somewhere else, for evil people cannot sleep until they have done their evil deed for the day. They cannot rest unless they have caused someone to stumble. They eat wickedness and drink violence! (Proverbs 4:14-17).

If you look up "whine" in a dictionary, you will discover that to whine is to "complain, moan, bleat and bellyache." Ugly—but all too familiar, isn't it? Ministry seems like the last place you should find a "bleater" or a "bellyacher." Not so. In fact, the road to vision is lined with them!

Vision is always met with at least two kinds of opposition. Some will oppose the dream God has given you because they do not understand the reasoning behind it. In short, they cannot see the vision. Your response to these people is to faithfully pursue the vision God has given you, continue to share that vision, then let God work. If they really want what God wants, either they will buy in—or they will leave, applauding what God is doing but understanding the vision God has given you is not the vision He has given them.

Then there are those who oppose vision because it robs them of their power. Vision is a holy calling—not a power trip. These people do not want to *understand* or *catch* the vision; they want to *hinder* the vision because it threatens their sense of importance and significance as power brokers in the church. Avoid these people! Vision is a sacred gift, a pearl, and a treasure from God. He expects us to guard it carefully.

As our church exploded in growth, it was quickly apparent—or so I thought—that we needed more space or the growth would stop. I have already shared how the leadership prayed and fasted for God's direction—and got it! The local high school, which was about two miles from the church, had just built a large new auditorium we could rent for two years while we built a bigger building.

The church leadership shared the vision; then they called the church to pray and fast before voting.

We soon discovered that one of the more vocal women in leadership did not want to move and was letting everyone know it. She made divisive phone calls through the week, gathered small groups after each service, hovering in secluded corners and hallways of the auditorium to voice her opposition and, in short, set herself and as many others as she could persuade against the vision.

The day of the vote finally came, and I was honestly hoping to avoid this particular "whiner." God had another plan. In fact, she was waiting for me by the sanctuary door. "Well, dear," she said, "we'll just see what happens tonight and who is really in charge around here, won't we?" Now, I have to admit that my first thoughts were not good ones—to say the least. In fact, they were just plain nasty. I can be so human! I counted to ten, prayed, took a deep breath, counted and prayed some more, and finally responded, "I already know who is in charge. What will happen tonight is that God's vision for this church will be done. And those who are willing to be part of that vision will stay, while those who want to hinder the vision will leave." She left. We stayed, and God's vision stood firm. Avoid the whiners!

Lesson Four: Never Lose Sight of the Vision

> Look straight ahead, and fix your eyes on what lies before
> you (Proverbs 4:25).

Vision originates with God, flowing from His heart to ours and then back to His heart as a sweet-smelling aroma. Vision is eternal. When we seek, find, and commit to that vision, God uses it as a vehicle for change. God gives vision for one reason only—to save the seeking heart. We can get so wrapped up in the "mechanics" of the vision that we lose sight of the vision itself and the reason God gave it—that lives and destinies might be changed through the power of the Holy Spirit at work.

After all, we are in ministry. We have important schedules to keep—and blinders in place, missing those who are hurting or lonely, stranded and wounded on the road of life. Desperate people who simply need a smile or a word of encouragement are either overlooked or viewed as unwelcome intrusions and unwanted interruptions to our very important "To-Do List" of religious activities. Schedules become a sacred icon, appointment books our dictator, and church programs our purpose. My heart breaks as I wonder how many broken lambs are still searching for a Shepherd because I was so wrapped up in ministry that I failed to be wrapped up in Him and His vision to rescue the lost.

> The enemy would love nothing more than to see us become distracted from God's vision by spending our time in putting out ministry fires set by those who oppose that vision.

The enemy would love nothing more than to see us become distracted from God's vision by spending our time in putting out ministry fires set by those who oppose that vision. We then become little more than damage controllers and emotional firefighters instead of God-ordained keepers of the vision. Don't allow anyone to steal your dreams. Don't let anyone sidetrack you or get in the way of God's vision at work in you and your ministry.

Lesson Five: Stay in the Word

> Don't forget or turn away from my words (Proverbs 4:5).

During the early days of transition at our church, it seemed as if every day was swirling with change. The turmoil seemed endless. I grew up in a very traditional church, so every change was a stretch for me, the woman who married "Mr. Transition" himself. I was certain of the vision, but was just as certain I did not like the price the vision required. I wanted everyone to like me. I wanted everyone to be happy and stay at Flamingo Road forever. I wanted everyone to love my husband and recognize his heart for God.

During a morning walk, I took the opportunity to voice my "wants" and protests to God, listing every change I didn't like. God stopped me in my tracks with words that silenced every complaint.

Mary, you have mistaken religious traditions for spiritual truths. Lay them all down. I will show you which ones you can pick up and which ones you can't.

The years of transition at Flamingo Road redefined my life. The Word of God became the hub of the wheel for me, the unchanging center that brought stability to my soul when everything around me was shifting. I truly learned that God's Word endures. "You have been born again…through the living and enduring word of God" (1 Peter 1:23 NIV). In this verse, "enduring" means "continuing forever." Vision is eternal—it flows from the lessons of yesterday through the challenges of today and into the promise of every to-morrow. Vision feeds on the Word of God. To pursue a new dream and follow a fresh vision, we must saturate our lives with His truth. It is the compass of vision.

Lesson Six: Increase Your Prayer Life

> Do not be anxious about anything, but in everything, by prayer and petition, with thanksgiving, present your requests to God (Philippians 4:6 NIV).

A vision must be bathed in prayer, because the strength to follow God's vision is a direct result of incessant prayer. There is power and boldness that comes through intimacy with God that can come no other way. We cannot "listen carefully" or "do what He says" unless we pray. Prayer brings everything into focus and clarifies a vision.

As women in ministry, we must be very careful to choose the right backdrop against which we live, love, and serve. Our backdrop is eternity, not the urgent demands of a pagan world. Our backdrop is an old rugged cross and an empty tomb—not the pharisaical prison constructed by power brokers in ministry.

My favorite words in the Bible are "but God." Those two words create an eternal focus that changes everything. Vision requires us to take the long look, refusing to fix our gaze on the "little things" meant to divert us from the main thing. Our glance must be on the circumstances of life while our gaze is on Him!

When we put prayer into place as a spiritual discipline, ministry will be the joy God intended, and fear will yield to peace. Does that mean we will float through each day without facing trials, defeats, enemies, or impossibilities? No, but it does mean that the backdrop against which we view those challenges will be replaced with His holy vision and the truth that He is enough.

Lesson Seven: Take Care of Your Home

> Encourage each other and give each other strength
> (1 Thessalonians 5:11 NCV).

I believe women are the thermostats of the home. When it comes to family, we are all women in ministry because our greatest opportunity to serve God begins at home. We can build a large church, invest countless hours in ministry, carve out impressive venues of recognition, and even attain fame in religious circles, but if our family is broken, our ministry is bankrupt no matter how good it looks on the outside. We find it easy to serve others instead of serving those we call "family." How often do we force our families to be content with the leftovers of our time and energy spent in ministry? I am sometimes guilty of giving my all at a speaking event, then crawling home, exhausted and spent, with little or no emotional energy set aside to serve my family.

I know the time and energy demands of ministry are endless, but when we serve our family, we are serving God. Tithing our time in service to family is just as important as tithing our money in giving. God will multiply and stretch our time just as He multiplies and stretches our money. Right priorities can so quickly be buried under an avalanche of church activities and ministry opportunities. If our homes and families operate in chaos, our ministries are an affront to the heart of God. Strong words, I know, but I am convinced that our greatest calling as women in ministry is lived out on the mission field of home.

One of the churches where Dan and I served seemed determined to fill every night of the week with some activity—a committee meeting, a choir rehearsal, a youth Bible study—all good things. But when you have two preschool children who are practically paying rent to live in the church nursery, something is wrong somewhere.

It had been a frenzied day. I was exhausted—both kids were worn out with no relief in sight. The phone rang. "Honey, I won't be able to make it home before visitation tonight," Dan said. He sounded so tired that I could not muster up one ounce of anger. Instead, I shifted into overdrive—snatching both kids off of the backyard swing and away from neighborhood friends, plopping them in the bathtub for a quick rinse, ramming limbs into clean clothes, and shoving food into little mouths before firmly depositing the two in their car seats. Off we went to church—again! At a stop sign, I glanced in the rearview mirror at two miserably silent children, tears streaming down their sad little faces. I heard His voice, *Mary, what are you doing, and who are you doing it for?* My heart broke. Turning the car around, I headed for home, saying, "Hey, guys! Would you like to go home, put on your pajamas, make some cookies, and watch a movie with me?" Cheers and clapping erupted from the backseat as tears gave way to smiling faces and laughter and giggles filled the air. I still remember that precious night of ministry!

As women in ministry, we delight in finding creative ways to touch hearts and are passionate about introducing those hearts to God's love, forgiveness, and transforming power. But I wonder how many of us miss the hungry hearts that greet us each morning across the breakfast table, wait for us to come home each night, or silently long for us to somehow convince them that they really are not total failures, unworthy and unwanted, but are, in fact, special in the eyes of God. How easy it is to lose focus and scramble priorities! We get so busy doing such good things and miss one of the highest things God created us to do—family.

My public ministry is only as valid as my private life. Family is the perfect framing for God's highest work, the litmus test for authentic ministry, and our greatest opportunity to meet needs in His name. When Danna was a little girl, one of her favorite activities was to color in what she called her "special" coloring book. It had several "special" pages, one in particular being a dull gray picture of a butterfly. Frankly, I couldn't understand her excitement. When I asked why she liked that picture so much, she grinned and said, "Watch, Mommy!" She rubbed her little hands together to create warmth, then laid her warmed hands on the butterfly drawing. The touch of her hand caused the special inks to react, and the dull gray was transformed into a vivid rainbow of color.

Everyone is hungry for the warm touch of someone who cares—a word of kindness, an act of compassion, a hug of encouragement. I believe God created the family to be the place where that hunger is best satisfied. Yet I am amazed we can stand in silence, watching homes, marriages, and families disintegrate before our very eyes. Silence is agreement—and no matter where or how we serve God, if we do not embrace family needs and issues, our ministry is incomplete and shortsighted.

Dan and I were so busy taking care of a fast-growing and highly visible church that we nearly lost "us." When we realized we were slowly slipping away from each other, we packed a bag, grabbed the kids, and headed to the beach for a weekend retreat. After hours of talking, playing, and praying, we made a commitment to God and to each other. We had one year—one year to balance priorities or leave the ministry. During that year, we made major changes that strengthened our home and marriage—changes that authenticated our ministry at Flamingo Road Church. Do not sacrifice your family on the altar of any church or ministry. One day, we will all stand before Him as keeper of the family He has given us. Will He be pleased? Will He say, "Well done"? Will our family stand and bless us? Whatever you do during times of transition, take care of your home.

Lesson Eight: Inspire Fun and Laughter

> I have told you these things so that you can have the same joy I have and so that your joy will be the fullest possible joy (John 15:11 NCV).

We were made to be vessels that contain His joy! We choose our perspective on life and in ministry. Perspective then determines attitude. From attitudes come actions that determine success or failure as well as quality of life and level of power in ministry. Paul is serious about joy when he writes, "Celebrate God all day, every day. I mean, revel in him!" (Philippians 4:4 MSG) Paul is calling us to party! That's right! We are to celebrate God every minute of every day for as many days as we have. "Revel" means "to party, to raise the roof" or, as my Mama would say, "Paint the town red." New dreams create new life and a fresh excitement in serving God. At the heart of vision is joy.

It is so easy to lose sight of the joy that comes from serving God and settle for happiness that comes from serving self. We assume that the demands of life and ministry make it hard to be happy when, actually, happiness is not what Paul is talking about at all. Happiness is a cheap imitation of true joy, depending totally upon man-made circumstances, while joy is an inside job, depending totally upon God's presence in the midst of life itself. Nehemiah 8:10 reminds us that "the joy of the LORD is your strength" (NIV). Remember, joy is not a feeling but rather a chosen perspective of recognizing God is in control.

Transition can be extremely stressful, and we all know that stress is deadly! I love the story of a woman who accompanied her husband to the doctor's office. After a thorough examination, the doctor called the wife into his office…alone. "Your husband is seriously ill," he began. "He has a very grave disease, and any kind of stress will kill him." "Is there anything I can do?" the woman asked. The doctor responded, "Every morning fix him a healthy breakfast and make sure he's in a good mood. Prepare nutritious meals, give him daily back rubs, and insist that he watch his favorite sports shows every night. Wear sexy lingerie and make love to him several times a week. In other words, satisfy his every whim. If you do this for the next year, I think he will live." On the way home, the husband asked his wife, "What did the doctor say?"

With great sadness she answered, "Honey, I'm afraid the doctor said you're going to die!"

Fun and laughter are spiritual disciplines. Joy is a response to the truth that God is in control! Proverbs 15:15 promises, "A cheerful heart has a continual feast" (NASB). This verse depicts an ongoing celebration—no matter what! No matter how rough the waters of transition get, we can still experience joy. No matter what outer circumstances suggest, our inward perspective can reflect joy. No matter what others say or do, we can and are called to pursue God's vision—joyfully.

Lesson Nine: Own the Lessons

> Getting wisdom is the most important thing you can do! And whatever else you do, get good judgment (Proverbs 4:7).

Ivory soap is the "soap that floats," but it wasn't always that way. Years ago, this soap was just another brand among many, until a factory foreman made a mistake. He left a fresh batch of soap in the cooking vat and went to lunch. When he was late getting back, the soap overcooked. The foreman frantically examined it. It seemed to clean the same—it was just lighter. He could either report the mistake and risk being fired, or he could make the best of it and ship the soap out as if nothing had happened. He shipped it out—with surprising results. Instead of complaints, the company was deluged with orders for this new "floating soap," and the foreman was promoted.

Some lessons are learned through successes we consider "victories," while others are learned in those defeats we consider "mistakes." God works through both. Success is measured not only in achievements, but in life lessons learned and owned. The transition process of Flamingo Road Church taught me that

- vision demands a radical obedience
- vision produces a holy passion

- vision fuels tenacious commitment
- vision defines clear purpose
- vision generates boldness
- vision gives new dreams
- vision transforms lives

As a longtime resident of southern Florida, I used to consider hurricanes to be mistakes of nature. However, I recently discovered hurricanes are necessary to maintain a balance. We all know the devastation these monstrous storms can cause. Yet scientists tell us hurricanes are tremendously valuable because they do a lot to break up the excess heat that builds up at the equator. In fact, hurricanes are indirectly responsible for much of the rainfall in North and South America. In spite of the suffering they cause, it seems that their absence would lead to even greater disruption and suffering.

Vision is filled with powerful life lessons. Some lessons come wrapped in light, while others ride the waves of darkness. Regardless of how they come, God uses them for good in our lives. We will never experience the power of God in ministry until we own each and every lesson that vision holds.

Lesson Ten: Never Give Up

> Mark out a straight path for your feet; then stick to the path and stay safe (Proverbs 4:26).

I am convinced that God entrusts His vision to those who will see it through. Don't ever give up on the vision God has given you. Be faithful to that calling until the day comes when you can place it back in the Father's hands and say, "Lord, here is the dream, the vision you gave me. I did what you called me to do. I never gave up."

> Since we are surrounded by such a great cloud of witnesses, let us throw off everything that hinders and the sin that so easily entangles, and let us run with perseverance the race marked out for us (Hebrews 12:1 NIV).

I am sure that God who began the good work within you will keep right on helping you grow in his grace until his task within you is finally finished on that day when Jesus Christ returns (Philippians 1:6 TLB).

Vision is God's "good work" entrusted to us, as women in ministry. It is His to give, His to empower, and His to keep. We are to "throw off" everything that would keep us from pursuing vision as we run the race He has set before us. When we do, we will experience God's power at work in our ministry.

How to Pursue God's Vision

Key verse: "Let your heart therefore be wholly devoted to the Lord our God, to walk in His statutes and to keep His commandments, as at this day" (1 Kings 8:61 NASB).

Key truths: I believe one of the main reasons we balk at pursuing vision is because we struggle with change, a struggle that is rooted in the fact we are not wholly devoted to God. I once read a Canadian road sign that said, "Be careful which rut you choose. You will be in it for the next 100 kilometers." My husband often says a rut is simply a grave with both ends knocked out. While ruts are both comfortable and predictable, they are also places filled with death.

Vision brings life and embraces change. Vision requires a fierce and ruthless examination of priorities. Priorities are not merely lists of activities completed or goals achieved, but candid reflections of our heart desires and level of obedience to God. Vision can scramble priorities and wreak heavenly havoc with established plans and life patterns, a frightening scenario for those of us who find great comfort in ministry "boxes." If we could just keep everyone and everything stuffed into one of our tightly lidded and "safe" ministry boxes, we could maintain control.

I love order! Organization is high on my list of coveted aspects of ministry. But when it comes to vision, there is no room for systematic or mundane spirituality. We must be willing to pursue vision, knowing that change is part of that pursuit.

Application steps:

- What new dream or vision is in your heart—now?

- How is God preparing you to carry out that vision? Look for specific direction and any steps of obedience He is asking you to take. Record those steps:

_____

_____

_____

- Prayerfully consider each step of transition listed below. Beside each step, record one new truth or insight gained from this chapter.

  T Take hold of emotions _____

  R Recruit a support team _____

  A Avoid the whiners _____

  N Never lose sight of the vision _____

  S Stay in the Word _____

  I Increase my prayer life _____

  T Take care of my home _____

  I Incite fun and laughter _____

  O Own the lessons _____

  N Never give up _____

- Which one of the above steps do you need to take today? Why?

Memory verse: "I am sure that God who began the good work within you will keep right on helping you grow in his grace until his task within you is finally finished on that day when Jesus Christ returns" (Philippians 1:6 TLB).

Reflection point: _So many women in ministry are imprisoned by feelings of inferiority. And the results are always disastrous. Constructive criticism is perceived as an emotional attack. Jealousy burgeons as others receive the accolades we desperately crave. Decisions are made and a course of ministry is determined so fragile egos can be fed, excluding God's plan and purpose._

Comparison reigns as a false idol in the attempt to validate worth and success. Inferiority crosses over to pride, and sin reigns.

Record any thoughts or fresh insights concerning the above statement:

_____

_____

_____

Power verses:

Praise the Lord, all you nations. Praise him, all you people of the earth. For He loves us with unfailing love; the faithfulness of the Lord endures forever. Praise the Lord! (Psalm 117:1-2).

You, my son Solomon, acknowledge the God of your father, and serve him with wholehearted devotion and with a willing mind, for the Lord searches every heart and understands every motive behind the thoughts (1 Chronicles 28:9 NIV).

The Lord is your security. He will keep your foot from being caught in a trap (Proverbs 3:26).

One new truth:

_____

_____

_____

V	Victorious
I	Insight
S	Surrendered
I	Idols
O	Overcoming
N	Never-failing

Broken
into Beautiful
A Life Story by Gwen Smith

Gwen Smith, *owner of Audio 31 Music (www.gwensmith .net), is a gifted songwriter, award-winning recording artist, and dynamic worship leader. Gwen has independently recorded four CDs. The song "Broken into Beautiful" is on her most recent CD project,* Because. *She is married to Brad, has three children, and is a worship leader for Proverbs 31 Ministries (www.proverbs31.org).*

My story is for the woman in ministry who has been to the depths of emotional isolation. It's for the woman whose life has been uprooted from everything familiar, living out of boxes while waiting for the moving truck to deliver her worldly belongings to a new home and foreign city. My story is for the woman who bravely puts on her lip gloss and plasters a protective smile on her face because the thought of actually revealing her struggles is overwhelming. This story is about the ongoing transformation of who I am *in* Christ and who I am called to be *for* Christ.

I met Jesus when I was nine years old. God not only gave me salvation, He gave me a gift to sing, and at the age of fourteen, called me to serve Him in ministry. I didn't know exactly what the specifics would be, but I knew I would sing for Him. It soon became apparent that my local church and community were the places God wanted me to hone my craft and seek His heart. I began writing songs, tucking them away from the world in a safe little folder. After all, they were just thoughts and songs for me.

I wish I could testify I made all the right decisions and did all the right things in preparation for ministry, but I can't. I have experienced seasons of intense growth in Christ and seasons of miserable failure. Mistakes have altered the very fabric of my life. The pain occasionally still lingers from those mistakes, but the blood of Jesus covers each memory with a blanket of love and forgiveness.

My early to mid-twenties were filled with ministry opportunities. I sang, worshipped, grew in my faith, and married. My husband, Brad, and I purchased our first home in Ohio, where we lived, as my career in the business world successfully unfolded. I was faithful with my talents and enjoying life.

After I gave birth to our first son, Preston, a whole new chapter of life began as I tried to balance diaper changes and feedings with marriage, housekeeping, social engagements, and ministry commitments. I had definitely entered the world of "Wonder Mom." No problem was too big, and no opportunity to serve was turned down. I was gaining momentum, and the wall was getting closer.

With a second child on the way, we moved…again…closer to Brad's work. Four weeks after Hunter was born, my world was rocked by a phone call saying my father was ill and might not make it through the night. That phone call set in motion a series of events that led me to ask God if I was doing what He created me to do. He began to stir my heart in a new way, reminding me of His calling on my life, nudging me—and not so gently, I might add—to expose my private lyrics and songs to a world I narrowly viewed as harsh and critical. I told Him I would *sing* for Him, but was not thrilled about sharing my intimate prose with others. He corrected me with the reminder that they were His songs, not mine. I surrendered, saying, "Okay, God, but this is on Your shoulders!" Praise God, He has strong and broad shoulders.

In the summer of 2000, my first CD was released, I was pregnant with our third child, and Brad accepted a job promotion that would take us to another state. Tension and stress became close friends, and I would soon meet a devastating enemy named brokenness. The moment I said yes to God, all that had been comfortable and familiar was stripped away. We had been in our second house for two years and I had three babies and a new ministry when we moved to a desert called Philadelphia, a place where I would *have* to trust Him.

Broken became my middle name. I had to hang up my microphone and spread my motherly wings to protect and nurture the babies in my nest. Bible study became a vital link to both God and other women. His Word began to birth new songs in my heart, and although I wasn't serving in music ministry, I was writing. Nine months after our move, I stepped back into music ministry on a very part-time basis. Six months later, Brad shared the news that his boss wanted him to take over a territory in Syracuse, New York. As we once again packed boxes, questions danced around in my mind. Had I heard Him wrong? Why in the world would God call me to a task and then herd me across the country like a nomad's cow?

The Syracuse summers were lush, but the winters were long. I was blessed with deep friendships, intense Bible studies, and godly leadership from the worship pastor at our new church. As a family, we began to immerse ourselves in the community, even though we knew we would probably not live there forever. While I was becoming more vulnerable in my songwriting, I was becoming less transparent in my friendships. I became the "Queen of Walls."

Seventeen months later, we moved to our current home— Charlotte, North Carolina—where I have begun to see God's plan unfolding in my life. Again, it is not what I had anticipated. He has rekindled the flame of my call to ministry and has stoked the fire with big logs. I am learning to be more transparent in friendships. I understand more and more each day there are risks involved in any worthy pursuit. Most of all, I see that if I had never been removed from my comfortable life in Ohio, I would not have experienced the brokenness necessary for authentic, vulnerable ministry. The price has been high but the rewards have been higher. I am now chasing His call on my life aggressively and drawing my strength from the deep well of compassion. There are still days when I feel overwhelmed, but I take comfort in knowing I walk with the "Paver of all roads" and He knows the way.

A postscript from Mary: I just have to jump in here. Gwen gave her life story the same title as a wonderful song she wrote, "Broken into Beautiful." The first time I heard that song, I realized that brokenness is not only the theme of Gwen's story but the very fabric of my own journey as well. As with Gwen, the most beautiful parts of my life were forged in the most broken times of my life. I've previously mentioned my two-year battle with clinical depression, which delivered me to the bottom of a deep, dark pit as my carefully built world caved in around me. I found myself imprisoned in a bottomless pit of pain and darkness, terrified and utterly broken. I had no idea how I had fallen into that sinkhole, but the more frightening reality was, I saw no way to escape.

Somewhere along the way, my outward journey had become more important than my inward journey. I was so wrapped up in ministry that I forgot to be wrapped up in God. I spent my whole life trying to earn His favor and prove my worth. I lived and ministered as if the only way to make Him and everyone else love me was to render a stellar performance, especially in the spiritual arena! That faulty thinking led to wrong priorities, unrealistic expectations, frustrating ministry, and a broken life...mine!

But brokenness yielded a life-changing truth. God doesn't love me because I'm so lovable. He loves me because He *is* love and no one can take my place in His heart. God empowers what He calls us to do. When we step out of that empowerment, we step into our own strength, depending upon our own limited resources.

Those resources are soon depleted, and darkness viciously closes in.

As God and I sifted through the broken parts of my life, we faced experiences I had carefully locked away—until they slammed into my heart and mind with staggering pain! An alcoholic father. A family doctor and friend who molested me. Loneliness and rejection. Haunting failures and unreasonable fears. It seemed as if the floods of poisonous memories would never end! But they did. And in their place, God brought fresh purpose and new dreams.

I know that many of you are wounded, desperately clinging to your last sliver of hope, almost ready to give up. Hang on, friend. God can and will heal your brokenness, as He did mine. He can and will transform your life into a trophy of grace and beauty.

Habit 5:

Opt for Peace

A little girl and her father were taking a walk one night. They lived in the country on a remote farm far from the neon signs and illuminated billboards of the city. The night was still and dark, cloaked in reverent silence. Lightning bugs danced through the tall grass in silent celebration of life and light.

Father and daughter walked in comfortable silence, enjoying the time together. With a sigh of contentment, the little girl lifted wonder-filled eyes toward the heavens. A host of winking stars filled the night skies as crickets and frogs joined in their worship of the Creator God. Overwhelmed by the night's beauty, the little girl exclaimed, "Oh, Daddy! If the wrong side of heaven is so beautiful, I wonder what the right side looks like!"

We live on the wrong side of heaven. This world is not our home—it's a broken place filled with broken people. Even so, we can live at peace in this foreign land for a while, knowing that home is waiting. We can celebrate *here* because of what we have *there*.

141

Peace and power go hand in hand. If we want to experience the power of God in ministry, we must first experience His peace. You may be thinking, *Peace? Never heard of it. What is it, and where do I go to find it?* Women in ministry constantly amaze me as they juggle the relentless demands of their calling, family, marriage, church, relationships, health, time, energy, finances, and just plain life! Life is so…daily!

For many years, I evaluated my personal worth on the basis of how successful I was in ministry. How successful I was in ministry was determined by how busy I was…ministering! God, in His infinite mercy, shut the door, turned off the lights, and said, "Enough!" It was time for a lesson in peace.

> Powerful ministry is marked by peace. We work hard at peace, yet many of us struggle to experience peace not only personally but in the ministry to which God has called us.

Darkness came. Dreams vanished, and in their place came an incredible emptiness and unspeakable pain. The weight of ministry was too much, so I laid it down. For two years, I sat in darkness at the feet of my God, pouring out years of hoarded frustration and amassed pain, learning the precious truths that would redefine my calling and thrust me into the most powerful ministry of my life. It was there, for the first time in my life, I learned the true meaning of peace.

When our daughter, Danna, was in the seventh grade, homework was not her favorite activity in life. Still isn't! However, one night, Dan and I came home to find her sitting at the kitchen table, laboring over homework. We concluded that miracles really do still happen!

After dinner, Danna excused herself from the table and went back to her homework. In fact, she was working so hard that Dan and I became curious almost to the point of suspicion, so we quizzed her on what she was doing. "I'm writing a really important report on the condition of the world and how to bring peace. The winner gets to read it in front of the mayor and the whole school," she replied.

We were impressed. "Isn't that a big order for one student—to come up with a plan to make the world a peaceful place?" her father asked. "Don't worry, Dad," she answered. "There are three of us in the class working on it!" If only life were that simple. It rarely is.

Powerful ministry is marked by peace. We work hard at peace, yet many of us struggle to experience peace not only personally but in the ministry to which God has called us. Something is wrong. Somewhere along the way, we have lost our peace...or so it seems.

The apostle Paul wrote a letter to the Colossians, encouraging them to live a holy life, a life of peace. In the third chapter of his letter, Paul lists the actions the Colossians were to take in order to restore the peace they had lost. They are the same steps we must take today in order to experience the peace of God.

> As God's chosen people, holy and dearly loved, clothe yourselves with compassion, kindness, humility, gentleness and patience. Bear with each other and forgive whatever grievances you may have against one another. Forgive as the Lord forgave you. And over all these virtues put on love, which binds them all together in perfect unity. Let the peace of Christ rule in your hearts, since as members of one body you were called to peace. And be thankful. Let the word of Christ dwell in you richly as you teach and admonish one another with all wisdom, and as you sing psalms, hymns and spiritual songs with gratitude in your hearts to God. And whatever you do, whether in word or deed, do it all in the name of the Lord Jesus, giving thanks to God the Father through him (Colossians 3:12-17 NIV).

Step One: Understand What True Peace Is

> In Christ Jesus you who once were far away have been brought near through the blood of Christ. For he himself is our peace (Ephesians 2:13-14 NIV).

Back in the 1800s, a young man was being interviewed to be the pilot of a steamboat on the Mississippi River. The interviewer, doubtful that the seemingly inexperienced young man could possibly know or understand the dangers of the river, asked if he knew where all the rocks were. The young man confidently replied, "No, sir, I do not know where all the rocks *are,* but I do know where they *aren't.*" He got the job.

To understand what peace *is,* we must first understand what it is *not!* Peace is not the absence of conflict, not a lack of trouble, not even a scarcity of problems. Peace is not a feeling. Peace is a Person. Paul assures us that "Christ himself is our peace" (Ephesians 2:14 NCV). Peace is a calm confidence even in the midst of conflict or trials, and it can only be found in God. Jesus often told those who came to Him, seeking forgiveness, to "go in peace." "Go in peace" can be literally translated "go into peace." We cannot afford to miss this truth.

When we enter into a personal relationship with Jesus Christ, we enter *into* peace. True peace has nothing to do with human beings or human circumstances. True peace cannot be produced on a human level at all. In fact, any "peace" that can be conjured up is not authentic peace—rather, it is very fragile and will not stand up against the onslaught of everyday life and the demands of ministry. Peace is the result of God's presence and power at home within us. When the power of God is unleashed in a life, that life takes on certain characteristics: love beyond human capability, patience beyond human control, and peace beyond human understanding.

When I think of a peaceful person, I tend to think of someone motionless in silent, still, and prayerful meditation. Tranquility hovers, producing a hushed serenity. Not necessarily. The apostle Paul was a man of peace, and he was anything but tranquil and still. I get the impression that Paul lived as if a helicopter was always landing somewhere in his life. Beatings, imprisonment, persecution...you name it, and Paul experienced it. Still, his letters to the churches he served are filled with joy and peace. As women in ministry, we hunger for that peace but often experience pandemonium instead.

We serve a God of miracles, a God who longs to pour Himself out in infinite power and unshakable peace through those willing to step out in faith and obedience. I want to be a woman after God's own heart, dwelling in the center of His will, celebrating the streams of miracles flowing from His hand of power and His heart of peace.

While God's power is miraculous, we sometimes live as if we are spiritual beggars without hope and without purpose. Why? We do not understand and walk in the truth that God really does make His power and His peace available to us. The question then becomes how to tap into His power and peace. Romans 5:1-2 simply but powerfully says, "Since we have been made right in God's sight by faith, we have peace with God because of what Jesus Christ our Lord has done for us."

Peace is the condition of wholeness and the sense of well-being that comes from knowing God and being made right in His eyes. Peace is completely dependent upon His presence in us and His gift of eternal life. We come into this world with an ache in our soul, a longing in our heart, and a deep sense of being lost. When we find God, we find home. Peace immediately takes up residence in our hearts and we are eternally "found."

When our son, Jered, was a little boy, he and his dad often went for a walk after dinner while I put Danna to bed. One night, Dan decided to test Jered's sense of direction. "How far are we from home, son?" Dan asked. Jered answered, "Dad, I don't know." Dan then asked, "Well, where are you?" Again, Jered answered, "I don't know." Dan laughed. "Sounds to me like you are lost, son." Jered looked up at his father, grinned, and said, "Nope, I can't be lost. I'm with you." With God, we are at home and at peace.

Step Two: Be Willing to Let Peace Rule

> Let the peace of Christ rule in your hearts (Colossians 3:15 NIV).

Understanding peace does not guarantee the presence of peace. I can fill my days with so many appointments, tasks, meetings, and activities that peace disintegrates before noon. Paul encourages us to "let the peace of Christ rule" in our hearts. The word "rule" is an athletic term meaning "to preside at the games and distribute the prizes." Sounds like a day at the office to me!

In the Greek games, there were judges who rejected the contestants who were not qualified, and disqualified those who broke the rules. Today, we would call them "umpires," and the playing field of peace would be our hearts. "Heart" refers to "the center of one's being." Peace begins its reign in the center of our being, then works its way out into every nook and cranny of life and every facet of ministry—if we allow it to rule.

Admittedly, there are times in ministry when an umpire seems like a good idea, because many of us relish a good fight. We say we want peace, but not at the price of giving up control or surrendering personal agendas. We must stand firm in our resolve to pursue harmony and peace, even if it means giving up rights and yielding control.

Relationships in ministry must be committed to peace. It is difficult to wage war with someone who has laid down their weapons in an act of surrender. Ah, there's that dreaded word again—surrender. Surrender is the heartbeat of peace. The choice to surrender initiates the process of allowing peace to rule. I guess you could say the peace of God is our "umpire"—and in every situation, stands ready to make the calls that will lead us to rest in and trust Him. But first comes the choice to "let" peace rule. The work of peace is always unleashed by our choice, our invitation.

Step Three: Be Right with God

> Let the word of Christ dwell in you richly as you teach and admonish one another with all wisdom, and as you sing psalms, hymns and spiritual songs with gratitude in your hearts to God. And whatever you do, whether in word or deed, do it all in the name of the Lord Jesus, giving thanks to God the Father through him (Colossians 3:16-17 NIV).

The lakes in Florida are beautiful, but relatively shallow as well. Over the years, they fill up with the silt and mire that wash off the shore. In time, they accumulate two to three feet of mire and decaying vegetation at the bottom. Soon the mire begins to deprive the lake plants and fish of valuable oxygen, and eventually the lakes literally die. In order to halt this process, a program has been put in place to drain the lakes periodically and expose the mire. After it is exposed, workers come in and dredge the mire—restoring the lake bottom to its original condition. The lake water can then be raised and soon the lake, its vegetation, and its fish are thriving again.

Our lives are much the same. We need to regularly expose and eliminate the "mire" or sin in our lives, since peace is always realized in a right relationship with God. The more we seek God and the more we nurture our relationship with Him, the stronger our peace will grow. When we have a personal relationship with God, we also have access to all of God's power and all of God's peace. How much power we receive *from* Him and how much peace we experience *in* Him depends upon how right our relationship is *with* Him. A right relationship with God depends on several commitments we must make.

1. First Commitment: Be in the Word

> Let the word of Christ dwell in you richly… (Colossians 3:16 NIV).

In this verse, "dwell" means "to feel at home." Paul is conveying the idea that God's Word should be such a natural part of our lives that it comfortably dwells with us and feels at home in us. When a Soviet official was asked why a study of the Bible was frowned upon in his country and why those who dared to print and distribute the Bible were severely punished, he replied, "We find that the reading of the Bible changes people in a way that is dangerous to our state!" When God's Word is "comfortable" in us, it changes lives through us.

Our greatest source of power in ministry comes from knowing, embracing, and applying the Word of God. "The word of God is full of living power. It is sharper than the sharpest knife, cutting deep into our innermost thoughts and desires. It exposes us for what we really are" (Hebrews 4:12). God's Word cuts away sin and heals the deepest wounds as it guides, directs, and dispels darkness. How many times we have been through the Bible is not nearly as important as how many times the Bible has been through us.

If you visit Yellowstone National Park, you will be given a piece of paper by one of the rangers at the park entrance. On it, in big letters, is written the warning "Do Not Feed the Bears." But when you drive into the heart of the park, you will still see people ignoring the warning. When a ranger was asked what was so bad about feeding the bears, he answered, "You have only a small part of the picture." The ranger went on to describe how, during the fall and winter months, when few people visit the park, the park service personnel have to carry away the bodies of dead bears—bears who can no longer feed themselves. Christians who are frantic do not know how to feed themselves the Word of God, because a steady diet of truth produces peace.

2. Second Commitment: Be Accountable

Admonish one another with all wisdom (Colossians 3:16 NIV).

In this verse, "admonish" literally means "to warn, instruct, or correct." Paul is talking about obedience that is guarded by accountability. As John 14:23 states, how much we love God is measured by how much we obey God. "Jesus answered, 'If people love me, they will obey my teaching'" (NCV). Obedience is easier in an atmosphere of accountability—a fact that is especially true in ministry.

Dan and I learned countless life lessons while serving Flamingo Road Church, but one of the most important lessons was in the area of accountability. Hardly a week passed without a distressed phone call from some pastor or pastor's wife, asking for help in their marriage, their ministry, or their personal lives. The problems ranged from drug addictions and alcoholism to extramarital affairs, prodigal children, mishandling church funds, or...well, you name it! Every phone call served as a reminder to Dan and the pastoral team to be diligent in their efforts to maintain a ministry of integrity. Wooden office doors were replaced with glass doors. A professional counselor was hired to handle the mounting demands and need for ongoing personal counseling. Weekly staff meetings always included a time of holding each other accountable for time spent with children and dates with spouses, as well as blunt conversations concerning potential temptations or struggles.

Strict—and some people would say, "over-the-top"—guidelines were put in place. For example, no pastor was ever to be alone with any woman other than his wife. Each week, the staff meeting concluded with lunch at a nearby restaurant. At times, it would have been more convenient for one of the pastors to ride with one of the secretaries. It never happened. Dan took a lot of teasing about those rules, but I am convinced God honored them. Paul says we should correct each other, warn each other, and instruct each other. In other words, we are to make ourselves accountable to one another.

Wives, a personal word to you on this point: One of our privileges and responsibilities in marriage, as well as in ministry, is to be the guardian of the home and the marriage relationship. Do not underestimate the enemy. His goal is to destroy your home, your marriage, and your family. And he will do it in any way he can. I am adamant about screening the women who make counseling appointments with Dan or seem to be emotionally attached to him in any way.

One Tuesday morning, I decided to stop by the church office to see Dan. Seated in the waiting area was a beautiful young woman, almost wearing a very short and very tight dress. She did not seem happy to see me, judging from her "drop dead" glare. Warning bells went off in my spirit, so I quietly asked the receptionist who the woman was waiting to see. "She is waiting to see Dan. Her marriage is in trouble." When I asked why she wanted to see a pastor instead of our staff counselor, the receptionist's eyes said it all. "I made that suggestion when she called, but she only wants to see Dan." I don't think so!

I headed for my husband's office and walked in unannounced, interrupting a meeting with our executive pastor. "Honey, I will be glad to sit in on your next appointment," I sweetly but firmly offered. He knows me well and immediately realized my suggestion was, in reality, a statement of intent. I went on. "Or, I can check with Terry to see if he has an opening in his counseling schedule." Dan smiled, not fully realizing what was happening but knowing there was a good reason for my suggestion. When Terry agreed to see her, the woman quickly decided she really didn't need to see someone after all. I rest my case.

Affairs are neither scheduled nor planned. I have never met anyone in ministry who woke up one morning and thought, *You know, I think I'll have an affair today.* Over the years, I have personally confronted women, warned Dan about a dangerous emotional attachment I saw that he didn't, and, while teaching a series on marriage, stated from the pulpit that Dan Southerland is off limits to any woman except me. I believe the statement went something like this: "Dan belongs to me. I am the only right sexual option for him and will be glad to remove anyone who disagrees." If Satan can, he will destroy the marriage of a pastor, crippling a church in the process. The world is certainly not the friend of marriage, but God certainly is.

We just planted several pine trees in our front yard. I was concerned they were not growing straight even though we had planted them straight. One of our neighbors told me not to worry. Her words of plant-life wisdom ring true for us as women in ministry, "The winter winds are coming," she said. "The pines will grow against the wind, straightening themselves while gaining strength to survive the winter." Obedience and accountability strengthen us for the storms of life and ministry.

3. Third Commitment: Be Thankful

> Sing psalms, hymns and spiritual songs with gratitude in your hearts to God. And whatever you do, whether in word or deed, do it all in the name of the Lord Jesus, giving thanks to God the Father through him (Colossians 3:16-17 NIV).

To give God thanks is to praise Him. I am convinced a chosen attitude of thanksgiving and praise is an important part of peace. Praise is a deliberate choice to give God thanks—no matter what. The secret to praise is found in Colossians 3:17: "Whatever you do, whether in word or deed, do it all in the name of the Lord Jesus" (NIV). If we do everything as an offering to God, with the perspective that He alone is our audience, it is much easier to be thankful. But when we live for ourselves, for the praise and approval of man, or for any reason other than to please God, we will never be contented, and our hearts will never know peace.

Praise is powerful because it measures our problems against God's power, transforming stumbling blocks into stepping stones and freeing us from having to understand our circumstances. In short, praise tunes us in to the sovereignty and sufficiency of God. I have an ongoing list of "praise" verses I pray when my attitude drifts toward criticism and I am tempted to complain:

> Sing to God; sing praises to his name. Prepare the way for him who rides through the desert, whose name is the LORD. Rejoice before him (Psalm 68:4 NCV).

> You sit as the Holy One. The praises of Israel are your throne (Psalm 22:3 NCV).

> Give thanks in all circumstances, for this is God's will for you in Christ Jesus (1 Thessalonians 5:18 NIV).

Our choice to praise God transforms our everyday surroundings into a dwelling place for Him. We are His children. He not only longs for us to praise Him but has made praise part of His will for our lives. When we praise God, peace rules, and stress steps down.

I'm Too Blessed to Be Stressed!

I refuse to be discouraged, to be sad or to cry.
I refuse to be downhearted and here's the reason why:
I have a God who's almighty, who's sovereign and
    supreme;
I have a God who loves me, and I am on His team.
He's all wise and powerful; Jesus is His name;
Though everything else is changeable, My God remains
    the same.
I refuse to be defeated—my eyes gaze on ahead.
God has promised to be with me, as through this life I
    tread.
I'm looking past my circumstances to heaven's throne
    above.
My prayers have reached the heart of God. I'm resting
    in His love.
I give thanks to Him in everything. My eyes are on His
    face.
The battle's His, the victory mine; He'll help me win
    the race.
I repeat—I'm too blessed to be stressed!*

How often do we allow the disgruntled church member to keep us from praising God? What difficult ministry circumstance are we tolerating simply because we are afraid to step out in obedience and faith? Why are we so quick to placate whiners or tolerate joy thieves who stalk our every step? When we, as women in ministry, permit anyone or anything to deny us the joy of praise, we are authorizing the enemy to set our heart agenda. Practicing gratitude and making praise a habit is a fundamental exercise in spiritual obedience and always, always pleases God.

---

* Author unknown. Adapted.

My great example. The life of my favorite apostle, Paul, offers a sterling example of someone who faithfully practiced the attitude of gratitude despite any life circumstance or ministry trial. Humanly speaking, he had every right to be angry with God. After all, he was a faithful follower of God, giving up material wealth, forfeiting political power and enduring great pain because of his radical commitment to Jesus Christ. Yet he wrote the book of Philippians, a book of joy and gratitude, while under house arrest, awaiting his own trial and probable execution. "I have learned to be satisfied with the things I have and with everything that happens" (Philippians 4:11 NCV). What an amazing statement coming from a condemned man! It has certainly taken less pain and fewer trials to cause me to shake my ungrateful fist in the face of God, questioning His plan and purpose.

> There's a money-back guarantee on every promise of God. What a deal! Behind His every promise is the perfect and flawless integrity of God Himself.

Now—let me be "gut honest." In my darkest moments, from the bottom of a slimy pit teeming with doubt and fear, I not only questioned God's power but His very presence as well. I stood in the rubble of my broken life, blaming Him for the ruin. Yet His love for me never changed, and His commitment to me never wavered. How can I become a woman of perpetual joy, my heart forever filled with sweet, simple gratitude for what He has done in the life of this unlikely servant? I can do what Paul did.

Paul explains he "learned" to be content. In other words, Paul chose his attitude, training his mind and heart to select an eternal perspective when facing any challenge. "Learned" means "to be educated by experience." Paul is saying that all of his life experiences, good and bad, became his tutor in gratitude. Paul learned to be "content," a word that means "contained." Paul trained himself to focus on inner resources, those God resources deposited in his heart and soul, rather than outward circumstances. He chose to be grateful, to give God praise no matter what his outer circumstances might be. "Give thanks in all circumstances, for this is God's will for you in Christ Jesus" (1 Thessalonians 5:18 NIV).

Paul knew he could trust God. Paul counted on God to come through because He had always come through for him. You see, there's a money-back guarantee on every promise of God. What a deal! Behind His every promise is the perfect and flawless integrity of God Himself. "I will give thanks to your name for your unfailing love and faithfulness, because your promises are backed by all the honor of your name" (Psalm 138:2).

A chosen attitude. In some parts of Mexico, hot springs and cold springs are found side by side—and because of the convenience of this natural phenomenon the women often bring their laundry to boil their clothes in the hot springs and then rinse them in the cold ones. A tourist who was watching this procedure commented to his Mexican friend and guide, "I imagine they think old Mother Nature is pretty generous to supply clean hot and cold water here side by side for their free use, right?" The guide replied, "No, señor, there is much grumbling because she supplies no soap." So much of ministry hinges on our chosen attitude and perspective. Yes, we can choose joy! While our perspective of life and ministry is ours to resolve, God is faithful to help us along.

I am convinced that God entrusts trials to us, giving us the opportunity to rest in His promises and resolve to be grateful even in the midst of those trials! When we choose gratitude, we are choosing joy! When our heart is fixed on gratitude, we are choosing praise, enthroning God in the midst of the circumstance. I love this truth—that our praise actually prepares a place for Him to dwell and reside.

What an amazing opportunity trials offer—an invitation for God to reign. No matter how deep the valley, no matter how painful the wound, no matter how treacherous the road, our choice to praise God is an invitation for Him to come. And when He comes, everything changes. "You are holy, enthroned in the praises of Israel" (Psalm 22:3 NKJV). To be right with God and know His peace, we must be in the Word, we must be obedient, and we must be thankful.

Step Four: Be Right with Each Other

> As God's chosen people, holy and dearly loved, clothe yourselves with compassion, kindness, humility, gentleness and patience. Bear with each other and forgive whatever grievances you may have against one another. Forgive as the Lord forgave you. And over all these virtues put on love, which binds them all together in perfect unity (Colossians 3:12-14 NIV).

The world has its own system for working out conflict. It's called retaliation. God has a different plan for working out conflict. It's called restoration. In 1 Thessalonians 5:13, Paul instructs us to "live in peace with each other" (NIV). We are to "clothe ourselves" with certain characteristics as preparation for peace to rule. The characteristics we bring to relationships determine the level of peace in those relationships. That means deliberately planning for peace. Peace makes the decision to resolve conflict before conflict comes.

God calls us to unity, to be members of one body committed to peace. While the peace of God may be beyond our control and above our understanding, it can become a reality in our lives and ministry when we choose to reject every enemy of peace.

Two boys on the school playground were discussing a boy in their class. One of them remarked, "He's no good at sports." The other quickly responded, "Yes, but he always plays fair." The critical one added, "He isn't very smart." His friend answered, "That may be true, but he studies hard." The boy with the mean tongue was getting frustrated. "Well," he sneered, "did you ever notice how ragged his clothes are?" The other boy kindly replied, "Yes, but did you ever notice they're always clean?" The first boy threw his hands up in frustration and walked away shouting, "It's impossible to talk to you!" Adopt the "Yes, but" philosophy in ministry and you will quickly find that the enemies of peace will avoid you like the plague.

For several years, I taught third grade in the public school system. Every student in every class knew that one of my pet peeves was tattling. In fact, I made a long tail out of construction paper, wrote "tattle-tail" on it, and pinned it to the bulletin board behind my desk. Every time a child came to me with a negative comment about another student, I simply pointed to the hanging "tail" and asked, "Are you sure you want to say those words?" Nine times out of ten, the reminder stopped them cold. So when the gossips call, refuse to entertain their caustic words. When conflict arises, deal with it swiftly, refusing to leave the table until that conflict is resolved. Make integrity the benchmark of your life and ministry. Do not allow any conversation, meeting, or gathering to become a "bash those who aren't present" session. Zealously guard your tongue and carefully measure your words. Peace is at stake.

As women in ministry, the prayer of the psalmist should be our prayer as well: "May the words of my mouth and the meditations of my heart be pleasing to you, O Lord, my Rock and my Redeemer" (Psalm 19:14 NIV). We can be at peace when we understand what true peace is, are willing to let peace rule, and are committed to being right with each other and with God who is Jehovah Shalom, "I am your peace."

Studying It Out:
How to Opt for Peace

Key verse: "You, Lord, give true peace. You give peace to those who depend on you. You give peace to those who trust you. So, trust the Lord always. Trust the Lord because he is our Rock forever" (Isaiah 26:3-4 ICB).

Key truths: We cannot *live* in peace until we first *experience* peace. Peace grows from a heart contract with God—and as with any treaty, trust is an important consideration in forming the agreement. Peace simply cannot exist where there is no trust.

Many things weigh us down, but all of them can and must be given to God in order to experience peace. Trust initiates the relinquishment of every care and concern to God. As we allow Him to carry the weight of worry, the burden of pain, and the penalty of every sin, we will experience peace. The Father is waiting for us to turn from anything that would keep us from celebrating His stubborn love, His limitless forgiveness, and His unconditional acceptance. He stands ready to take the wrong things we have done and use them to help us live right. When we do…we will know peace.

You would think that ministry is just crammed full of peace. Yet I find so many women serving God while flailing in a self-made pressure cooker filled with anxiety and stress. Flawed trust is the problem. We don't fully trust God—to empower His plan in and through us, to supply every need—to be God! We rely upon our own abilities, strengths, and power because they are measurable and recognizable. As a result, we live in emotional pandemonium and minister from a spiritual deficit, when we should be prospering in peace. Right now, make a new commitment to God. Seek Him wholeheartedly and practice His presence, knowing that peace will follow.

Application steps:
- In your own words, define peace. Compare your thoughts to God's standards of peace.
- In what areas of your life and ministry does peace rule?
- Identify the "peace thieves" in your life. What steps do you need to take to eliminate and guard against those thieves?

- Are you right with God? Take a "silent retreat" to sit at His feet and evaluate the health of your relationship with God.
- Examine your relationships. Deal with any unresolved conflict.

Memory verse: "Peacemakers who sow in peace raise a harvest of righteousness" (James 3:18 NIV).

Reflection point: *Our choice to praise God transforms our everyday surroundings into a dwelling place for Him.*

Record any thoughts or fresh insights concerning the above statement:

_____

_____

Power verses:

I will heal my people and will let them enjoy abundant peace and security (Jeremiah 33:6 NIV).

The mind set on the flesh is death, but the mind set on the Spirit is life and peace (Romans 8:6 NASB).

It is better to eat a dry crust of bread in peace than to have a feast where there is quarreling (Proverbs 17:1 NCV).

One new truth: _____

_____

_____

P	Peace
E	Enthroned
A	At
C	Christ's
E	Expense

I Am Loved
A Life Story by Mary Nash

Mary Nash *is a chaplain with Youth for Christ as well as director of numerous support groups for women and teenage girls who are victims of abuse and cancer survivors. Mary is married, has two children, and is a lay leader at Flamingo Road Church in Ft. Lauderdale, Florida (donmarna@aol.com).*

I was 47 years old before I was willing to surrender my life of pain. I was so tired of carrying around the weight of physical, emotional, and sexual abuse—alone. Through hard emotional work, prayer, and choosing to accept the promises of God, I finally gave everything about me to God. The relief was beyond measure as I realized God loved me just the way I was. Jude 24 became a watchword for me: "[He] is able to keep you from falling and to present you before his glorious presence without fault and with great joy" (NIV). I understood that Jesus would present me to God as a spotless lamb, but it was difficult for me to accept His love. I had to overcome years of feeling that I was a dirty, worthless person who could not be loved by anyone, much less God.

As the youngest of 14 children, I was unwanted. Several times, my mother tried to harm me physically, and by the age of six, I was already a wounded soul. Life had been difficult from birth, but it suddenly got worse when my mother brought home a man who abused me sexually—for four years. My sense of worthlessness was complete.

When I was 13, God sent two women into my life with the good news that someone loved me just as I was. I felt drawn to their church, where I discovered Christian people who really cared about me and a God who loved me. When I asked Jesus to be the Lord of my life, my thoughts and actions slowly changed, and I grew in Him. Still, I never told anyone about the abuse I had lived with for so long. Instead, I stuffed it down and tried to forget it.

After finishing college, I married a wonderful man, had two great kids, and surrounded myself with Christian friends. Psalm 27:10 became an important promise to me, "When my mother and father forsake me, then the LORD will take care of me" (NKJV). But I couldn't forget the years of abuse from my mother and her boyfriend. The need to be a spiritually healthy mother and wife, as well as the hope that recovery was possible, drove me to see a Christian counselor. He was a kind, caring man, but I was still unable to talk about my abuse. I was ready to give up. But God works in wondrous ways on behalf of His children.

One day, my counselor added a watercolor painting to his office. It bore a striking resemblance to the home where I grew up. That single picture opened the floodgates, and all my past hurts came pouring out. For the first time in my life, I was able to talk about my pain. It didn't happen overnight, but slowly I was able to accept that little girl of long ago and understand she was a beautiful child of God. For the first time, I realized God had a purpose for me, a purpose that began to unfold when my counselor encouraged me to assist him with a support group for women who had been sexually abused as children. That first group was as difficult for me as it was for the other participants, but God used it as a catalyst of healing in my life. Since then, I have facilitated many groups, helping women of all ages come to terms with their own abuse while leading them to understand how much God loves them. Just sharing and talking has incredible healing power. It takes the terrible sting out of the problem and gives great freedom to the soul as the secrets become less important.

God recently revealed another purpose for my life when He directed me to a program for children who have been sexually abused and removed from their homes for their own protection. Telling my story to these children and allowing them to question me brings a sense of completeness and great joy to my life. Every time I visit them, I am reminded of how secretive I was as a child and how I never wanted anyone to know about my home life. Encouraging them to talk about their problems, think about the possibilities for their future, and risk letting God into their lives is the most important thing I can do for them.

My home church recently ordained me as a chaplain with Youth for Christ. I now have a prison ministry in the Juvenile Division of Dade and Broward County, Florida, that allows me to teach weekly Bible studies to girls who have been hurt and abused in their own homes. Some are hardened and need immediate intervention if they are to change the direction of their life. It is good for them to hear the stories of others who were hurt and going down a wrong road when God changed their lives. Almost every girl I have talked with has expressed her need for God and surrendered her life to Him. Prayer warriors pray for these girls to keep their commitment when they return to the same homes, schools, and friends who were part of their old lives.

None of this would be possible without people who care. The women who came to me as a teen changed my life. Now, other women help me carry out God's plan of changing lives. I could do nothing without their love, prayers, and physical presence in working with these young women.

I never dreamed God would take my broken soul, make me whole, and use all the bad in my life for good. My purpose is still unfolding, one day at a time. I have learned never to be surprised by what God asks me to do. I just want to be God's woman doing God's work wherever and whenever He calls.

Strive for Greatness

While at work, a woman received a frantic phone call from her babysitter saying her infant daughter was very sick. The woman quickly called her pediatrician, left work, and on her way home, stopped by the pharmacy to pick up a prescription the pediatrician had ordered. When she came out of the pharmacy, she realized her keys were locked in the car. Panic consumed her when she called home only to hear her daughter was worse.

Looking around for help, the now terrified mother spotted a coat hanger lying on the ground. She picked it up but had no idea how to use it to open the car door. By this time, she was desperate, so she bowed her head and fervently prayed for help. As she prayed, an old rusty car pulled up beside her, and out of the driver's side emerged a dirty, greasy, bearded man wearing a frayed biker skull rag. Out of time and options, the woman decided to be thankful for answered prayer.

In less than a minute, the stranger had taken the hanger and opened the car. With tears of relief cascading down her face, the woman hugged the man and said, "Thank you so much! You are a very nice man!" Quickly, the shabby angel shook his head. "Lady, I am not a nice man. I have been in prison for car theft and just got out an hour ago." Without hesitation, the thankful mother hugged the man again, closed her eyes, and sobbed out a fervent prayer: "Thank you, God, for sending me a professional!" The biker may have seemed an unlikely choice to many, but to the woman, he mattered. In her eyes, he was a roaring success and smacked of greatness.

> True success and greatness come only from God. He alone can empower ministry.

If we are honest, we can admit that we all strive for greatness in ministry but secretly wonder if the desire to be great is even a godly or right desire. We yearn to experience the power of God in ministry, mistakenly assuming it lies in our expertise, training, education, and experience. While each of those areas serves as a tutor in ministry, true success and greatness come only from God. He alone can empower ministry.

You may be surprised to know there is nothing wrong with the desire for success and greatness in the kingdom of God. James and John, two of Jesus' disciples, came to Jesus, asking that He grant them a place of honor. In short, they were asking Jesus to make them great in His kingdom:

> "Teacher," they said, "we want you to do for us whatever we ask." "What do you want me to do for you?" he asked. They replied, "Let one of us sit at your right and the other at your left in your glory." "You don't know what you are asking," Jesus said. "Can you drink the cup I drink or be baptized with the baptism I am baptized with?" "We can," they answered. Jesus said to them, "You will drink the cup I drink and be baptized with the baptism I am baptized with, but to sit at my right or left

is not for me to grant. These places belong to those for whom they have been prepared" (Mark 10:35-40 NIV).

You can imagine the reaction of the other ten disciples when they heard the outrageous request of James and John. Scripture tells us they were "indignant" and angry. Evidently, competition in ministry was alive and well—even then. Instead of censuring James and John for the request, as I would have, Jesus explains the decision is not His to make and then specifies the commanding cost of greatness in the Kingdom of God—total and sacrificial service.

> Jesus called them together and said, "You know that those who are regarded as rulers of the Gentiles lord it over them, and their high officials exercise authority over them. Not so with you. Instead, whoever wants to become great among you must be your servant, and whoever wants to be first must be slave of all. For even the Son of Man did not come to be served, but to serve, and to give his life as a ransom for many" (Mark 10:41-45 NIV).

Samson was a man who seemed naturally destined for greatness. Most people believe Delilah was the evil woman who interrupted that greatness and caused the fall of Samson, a noble man of God. I believe Delilah was just one more stop on the road of destruction foolishly traveled by Samson in his quest for greatness. You see, while both Samson and Delilah wanted to be great, both misunderstood what true greatness was and how it could be attained.

> Samson fell in love with a woman named Delilah, who lived in the valley of Sorek. The leaders of the Philistines went to her and said, "Find out from Samson what makes him so strong and how he can be overpowered and tied up securely. Then each of us will give you eleven hundred pieces of silver."

So Delilah said to Samson, "Please tell me what makes you so strong and what it would take to tie you up securely."

Samson replied, "If I am tied up with seven new bowstrings that have not yet been dried, I will be as weak as anyone else."

So the Philistine leaders brought Delilah seven new bowstrings, and she tied Samson up with them. She had hidden some men in one of the rooms of her house, and she cried out, "Samson! The Philistines have come to capture you!" But Samson snapped the bowstrings as if they were string that had been burned in a fire. So the secret of his strength was not discovered...

Day after day, she nagged him until he couldn't stand it any longer.

Finally, Samson told her his secret. "My hair has never been cut," he confessed, "for I was dedicated to God as a Nazirite from birth. If my head were shaved, my strength would leave me, and I would become as weak as anyone else."

Delilah realized he had finally told her the truth, so she sent for the Philistine leaders. "Come back one more time," she said, "for he has told me everything." So the Philistine leaders returned and brought the money with them. Delilah lulled Samson to sleep with his head in her lap, and she called in a man to shave off his hair, making his capture certain. And his strength left him. Then she cried out, "Samson! The Philistines have come to capture you!"

When he woke up, he thought, "I will do as before and shake myself free." But he didn't realize the LORD had left him.

So the Philistines captured him and gouged out his eyes. They took him to Gaza, where he was bound with bronze chains and made to grind grain in the prison. But before long his hair began to grow back.

The Philistine leaders held a great festival, offering sacrifices and praising their god, Dagon. They said, "Our god has given us victory over our enemy Samson!"

When the people saw him, they praised their god, saying, "Our god has delivered our enemy to us! The one who killed so many of us is now in our power!"

Half drunk by now, the people demanded, "Bring out Samson so he can perform for us!" So he was brought from the prison and made to stand at the center of the temple, between the two pillars supporting the roof.

Samson said to the servant who was leading him by the hand, "Place my hands against the two pillars. I want to rest against them." The temple was completely filled with people. All the Philistine leaders were there, and there were about three thousand on the roof who were watching Samson and making fun of him.

Then Samson prayed to the LORD, "Sovereign LORD, remember me again. O God, please strengthen me one more time so that I may pay back the Philistines for the loss of my eyes." Then Samson put his hands on the center pillars of the temple and pushed against them with all his might. "Let me die with the Philistines," he prayed. And the temple crashed down on the Philistine leaders and all the people. So he killed more people when he died than he had during his entire lifetime (Judges 16:4-9,16-30).

The lives of Samson and Delilah offer compelling insight into kingdom greatness and powerfully communicate the steps we must take as we strive for greatness in the eyes of God.

Step One: Respond to the Call of God

Manoah's wife went to him and told him what had happened. She said, "A man from God came to me. He looked like an angel from God...he said to me, 'You will become pregnant and will have a son. Don't drink wine

or beer or eat anything that is unclean, because the boy
will be a Nazirite to God from his birth until the day of
his death'" (Judges 13:6-7).

Samson was born for a special purpose, created to accomplish
a unique plan, and set apart by God for a life filled with promise.
Samson was a Nazirite, a name which comes from the Hebrew word
meaning "to separate" or "to consecrate." He did not first choose
God. God first chose him and even sent an angel to announce his
birth, which was the birth of a "miracle baby" since his mother was
unable to have children. "Samson" literally means "sunny, or bright-
ness." I can only imagine how much joy he must have brought his
parents, not to mention the Israelites as he fought to free them
from their enemies, the Philistines. God chose and called Samson
to initiate the battle for Israel's deliverance, and Samson responded
in obedience.

Greatness always begins with a response of obedience to the call
of God. Just as Samson was created for a special plan, so are we.
I love the promise of Ephesians 2:10: "God has made us what we
are. In Christ Jesus, God made us to do good works, which God
planned in advance for us to live our lives doing" (NCV). As women
in ministry, we diligently teach others the always amazing truth that
God loves them and, in response to that love, has created them with
a unique plan in mind. But when it comes to our own lives, we tend
to bypass that truth, choosing instead to create a logical plan—a
safer plan that we can tangibly calculate as both acceptable and do-
able in our own strength. The result is a lack of purpose, a void of
power—and many times, a quick exit from ministry itself.

God has "good works" for us to do. When we say yes to those
good works, we are taking hold of greatness. Service is always at the
heart of greatness. "Whoever wants to become great among you
must serve the rest of you like a servant" (Mark 10:43 NCV). Spiritual
greatness begins in a personal relationship *with* God that is lived out
in service *to* God. What we are is His gift to us, but how we serve
Him is our gift to Him.

It is not enough to be competent. We can take absolutely no credit for any talent, ability, or gift we possess. We have been invested with those gifts by God. Our responsibility is to manage and develop each gift, using it for God in order to make His kingdom prosper. When we pray for the Lord to use us, we are asking Him to do something He already wants to do and plans to do! When we respond to the call of God, we will naturally serve Him, choosing to take a first step on the road to greatness.

Step Two: Recognize Our Source of Strength

> I have never had my hair cut, because I have been set apart to God as a Nazirite since I was born. If someone shaved my head, I would lose my strength and be as weak as any other man (Judges 16:17 NCV).

Samson's strength came from God. His long hair and his unusual physical ability were outward displays of God's strength within him. Samson's great feats were widely known, a testimony to the presence and power of God at work in his life.

- He killed a lion bare-handed.
- He killed 30 Philistines at one time.
- He caught 300 foxes and tied torches to their tails.
- He killed 1000 men with the jawbone of a donkey.
- He carried off a city gate.
- He destroyed the Philistine building.

While God may not call us to wrestle wild animals or physically destroy formidable enemies, He does call us to step out in faith, in His power, and in blind obedience. Power will come as we go. "I can do everything with the help of Christ who gives me the strength I need" (Philippians 4:13). What a promise this verse offers—the picture of Jesus continually, faithfully depositing His strength in us, empowering His will for every step and allowing us to participate in eternal business. That is powerful ministry.

As I study the life of Samson, I am left with the distinct impression he was a man who had a great sense of humor and loved to have a good time—but didn't always take his gifts or his calling seriously. Even though the calling of God is a blessing beyond measure, our humanity makes it easy to lose the wonder of all God has done. The Psalmist warns, "Obey the LORD with great fear. Be happy, but tremble" (Psalm 2:11 ICB). In order to experience the power of God in ministry, we must understand that our only source of strength is God. Samson lost the awesome wonder and holy fear of God, growing numb to his own inadequacy, thinking his strength alone was enough. It was never enough for Samson and will never be enough for us.

God always demands an accounting of how we use His power and manage the gifts He has given us. Samson's heart filled with pride as he began to misuse all that God had invested in his life. When we continually recognize God as our source of strength, pride will die from lack of attention, and we will find ourselves one step closer to greatness in the kingdom of God.

Step Three: Take Charge of Our Wants

> Samson fell in love with a woman named Delilah...The leaders of the Philistines went to her and said, "Find out from Samson what makes him so strong and how he can be overpowered and tied up securely. Then each of us will give you eleven hundred pieces of silver" (Judges 16:4-5).

Samson's uncontrolled wants became a source of constant temptation, temptation that targeted his weaknesses and led to his ultimate demise. Delilah was only one of several women who seduced Samson. She was a prostitute, willing to sell herself to the highest bidder. When the Philistine leaders offered her an enormous amount of money to help them capture Samson, she quickly consented.

Desire for Wealth

Greed is a powerful "want" and is responsible for the downfall of countless men and women in ministry. Money is a good servant but a poor master. Martin Luther once said, "God divided the hands into fingers so that money could slip through." One of the wealthiest men who ever lived was John D. Rockefeller. Following his death, so the story goes, a reporter was interviewing Rockefeller's chief accountant and asked the pointed question, "How much did John D. leave? We know that he was very wealthy." Without hesitation, the accountant shot back, "Everything! He left everything!" We need to constantly be aware of the spiritual legacy we will leave behind, refusing to compromise the purity and integrity of that legacy by allowing greed to infiltrate our motives in ministry. Greed is a deadly master that is never satisfied.

After a Saturday-night worship service, my husband, Dan, was in his usual place down front, talking with those who had made a decision for Christ that night and meeting first-time visitors to Flamingo Road Church. As I looked over the crowd gathered around my husband, I noticed Jenna, the five-year-old daughter of our worship leader, sitting on the edge of the platform, patiently waiting for Dan. After several minutes, Jenna was obviously tired of waiting, spotted me sitting on the first row and evidently decided I would have to do.

Jumping off the stage, Jenna headed straight for me, grinning and pointing to her mouth. "Mimi, guess what? I lost a tooth!" Carefully examining the illustrious gap, I exclaimed, "That's great, Jenna! The tooth fairy will definitely come tonight!" She grinned, "Oh, he already came last night and brought me $5.00. So, my mom took me to the mall today and I bought lots of stuff!" Tooth loss has definitely inflated to a higher level over the years. "That's wonderful, Jenna," I exclaimed, giving her a big hug. She did not hug me back and, in fact, seemed disappointed. I was confused, obviously missing some important point. Jenna's next words explained it all. "Yes...but Pastor Dan always gives me money when I lose a tooth!" Ah, the truth comes out! Reaching for my purse, I pulled out a dollar and pressed it into Jenna's outstretched hand. With longing in her eyes, Jenna gazed at the dollar bill and softly said, "I wish this dollar was really five dollars so I could go back to the mall and buy more stuff." And there you have the heart of man. We were all born greedy and get worse—just like Delilah.

Desire for Recognition

There are all kinds of greed in life and in ministry. Delilah may have been lured into the plan for the destruction of Samson not only because of the money, but also by the fact the Philistine leaders were coming to her for help. After all, she was a woman, and in that culture she was certainly not considered a first-class citizen. Power is a controlling "want" and has been responsible for so much pain in ministry. In some ministry circles, power equals significance. Knowing God is not enough. Faithful service goes unrewarded— and the only thing that matters is how we play "the game." We have to know the "powers that be"—those who can make things happen and further our advancement up the ministry ladder. We need to be extremely careful that we don't believe "our own press," because ultimately, the only evaluation that really counts is the one God gives. Do not settle for the power and approval of man when you can have the power and approval of God.

Delilah was a prostitute who, for perhaps the first time in her life, had the chance to be recognized as someone important and powerful. She was an immoral woman. Samson was a chosen servant of God. Both were destroyed because they could not control their greed, their "wants." The Bible warns that uncontrolled desires always lead to sin and destruction: "A person without self-control is as defenseless as a city with broken-down walls" (Proverbs 25:28).

When God gave us the Holy Spirit and the Word of God, He gave us everything we need to live a life of victory, a life of abundance. To experience His power in ministry, we must choose Him above all others—not just once, but every minute of every day, joyfully exchanging our agenda for His, gladly relinquishing our will to His. We must constantly choose *against* the old nature and *for* the new nature granted when we surrender to the lordship of Jesus Christ. Internal civil war is the result—our old nature warring with the new nature for control. We must feed the nature we want to win and turn from old habits toward new ones.

The story is told of a man with a severe limp who was awaiting radical surgery to correct his disability. As the day scheduled for his operation grew near, he was admitted to the surgical unit and preparations for surgery were begun. Each morning, he hobbled down the hallway with the help of a walker, strengthening his legs for the approaching surgery.

Finally, the day of his surgery came, and he was rolled into the operating room. Although it was an intricate procedure, the surgeon felt sure he could restore the man to complete health. The surgery went as planned, and the surgeon was thrilled with the results. However, there was one problem. For nearly a year following surgery, the man continued to limp. During a routine checkup, one of the nurses who had followed the man's progress commented to the surgeon, "It's a shame the surgery was a failure." The doctor sadly responded, "The surgery was a great success. That man limps out of nothing more than habit."

Old habits die hard! Old patterns of sin are not easily destroyed, but they *can* be destroyed when we take charge of our wants, submitting them to the scrutiny of obedience.

In a sermon on sin, one preacher announced there were 789 different sins. A few days later, the mailman delivered 94 requests from members of his church asking for a list of those 789 sins. Maybe we need a "sin list" that will make us conscious of our weak areas, knowing they can easily become a foothold for the enemy. Being aware of vulnerable spots is a great hedge of protection in taking charge of our wants, making a commitment to obedience and striving for greatness.

Step Four: Refuse to Take Revenge

> The Philistines went up and camped in the land of Judah. The men of Judah asked them, "Why have you come here

to fight us?" They answered, "We have come to make Samson our prisoner, to pay him back for what he did to our people." Then three thousand men of Judah went to the cave in the rock of Etam and said to Samson, "What have you done to us? Don't you know that the Philistines rule over us?" Samson answered, "I only paid them back for what they did to me'" (Judges 15:9-11).

Samson fought the Philistines for 20 years, killing many of them and destroying much of what they had. The Philistines retaliated, and Samson was determined to get even. Anger and revenge consumed him and, as they always do, distracted him from the will of God. God's calling became Samson's personal battleground. Revenge became Samson's consuming passion, changing the direction of his entire life and ministry.

Delilah was also motivated by revenge. She hated the Israelites, the nation Samson was destined to lead. She did not worship God and viewed the Philistines' offer as her chance to take personal revenge on Israel. Revenge is so powerful because it is fueled by unresolved and uninhibited anger. When we are mistreated or hurt, we want revenge—not justice. Revenge never produces true justice. Only God can mete out justice, and He is very clear on the matter: "It is mine to avenge; I will repay. In due time their foot will slip; their day of disaster is near and their doom rushes upon them" (Deuteronomy 32:35 NIV). Anger actually gets in the way of God's justice! Mishandled anger works its way out in our lives in the form of revenge, and revenge always leads to retaliation instead of restoration. Ministry is no place for revenge.

> Opportunities for retaliation are everywhere! However, a heart of integrity, a life striving for greatness in the eyes of God, chooses restoration over retaliation every time.

When our daughter was just a toddler, she went through a brief phase of biting. Danna was, however, selective in the object of her taste tests. After all, what are brothers for? I was doing laundry one night, enjoying the quiet house, when a bloodcurdling scream launched me from my solitude into Danna's room. She and her brother were supposed to be playing a nice, quiet game of "Chutes and Ladders" while I worked, but I didn't remember screaming being part of that game.

When I reached her bedroom, I found Danna's mouth attached to Jered's arm as if it were a turkey leg. "Danna," I barked, "What are you doing?" I know. I am not too bright at times. Danna was obviously in mid-bite. However, my voice did startle her and, thankfully, she released her prey, evoking fresh howls of pain from Jered. I gently gathered him in one arm and not so gently gathered Danna in the other. "Danna, do not bite!" I firmly warned. "Don't cry, honey!" I crooned to Jered. "Your sister is too little to know biting hurts."

With Jered pacified and Danna distracted, I headed back to the kitchen and my quiet laundry. I was barely out of the room when I heard screaming again—but this time it was Danna. Rushing back in, I asked, "What happened?" The epitome of innocence, Jered sweetly explained, "Well, she knows it hurts now!" Admit it—retaliation is fun! I particularly love the thinking behind this old Chinese proverb: "If thine enemy wrong thee, buy each of his children a drum." Retaliation is always sin, and revenge is always wrong.

As women in ministry, we soon discover that hurt and pain are part of the job description and common to the calling. Opportunities for retaliation are everywhere! However, a heart of integrity, a life striving for greatness in the eyes of God, chooses restoration over retaliation every time.

Step Five: Build Relationships with Godly People

> Pursue faith and love and peace, and enjoy the companionship of those who call on the Lord with pure hearts (2 Timothy 2:22).

Samson was a loner. He seemed to have no one on earth who would encourage him or hold him accountable for the decisions he made. As a young man, he married a Philistine woman, a choice that could easily be viewed as a slap in the face of his parents. He sought out prostitutes. He lived with Delilah. Not only had Delilah lived with idol worshippers, she was a prostitute and involved in a conspiracy with the Philistines.

Great people surround themselves with great people, willing servants, whose every step and every thought is the result of a radical abandonment to God. If we really want to be all God wants us to be, we would be wise to seek out people who will not only love and encourage us on our journey, but who are willing to confront and correct us when we take a wrong turn. Godly people call us up higher. Great people challenge us. "As iron sharpens iron, so one man sharpens another" (Proverbs 27:17 NIV).

The people we choose to spend time with will either help us or hurt us. Like Samson and Delilah, we are tempted to surround ourselves with those who will approve our sin and even encourage us down the wrong path we are determined to travel. Their silence is agreement. They say the words we want to hear. These people will not encourage us toward spiritual greatness.

Several months ago, the wife of a pastor in the area called to ask for prayer concerning a close friend with whom she spent huge chunks of time. They had been friends for years, but every time they were together, this pastor's wife spent too much money, ate too much junk food and, more importantly, slipped into the verbal habit of being negative and critical of others. She realized she needed to end the friendship but also knew it would be hard because the friend was married to the chairman of deacons in the church where her husband was pastor. In her mind, the possible ramifications were vast. Still, I encouraged her to back away from this unhealthy relationship and begin seeking out friends who were willing to love her, as well as challenge her to be all she could be in Christ. We talked and prayed, but after hanging up, I had serious doubts she would actually end the friendship.

A few months later, I ran into this woman at the mall. She tackled me in a fierce hug, thanking me for encouraging her to end the problem friendship. It had been very hard, she admitted, but she went on to say that life changed when she began spending time with women who called her up "higher." "Mary, they love me just like I am, will call me on the carpet when I blow it, but are my greatest cheerleaders too!" Yes—we become like the people with whom we spend the most time. If you want to be great in God's kingdom, become the servant of all and surround yourself with people who want the same thing.

Samson realized he had sinned and turned his back on the greatness for which he was born. Nevertheless, in the last moments of his life, he asked for forgiveness and once again brought honor to God by his obedience. I sometimes wonder how the story would have ended if Samson had made different choices, employing the wisdom only God can give. "Treasure wisdom and it will make you great; hold on to it, and it will bring you honor" (Proverbs 4:8 NCV). The lives of Samson and Delilah offer us great wisdom. What we do with that wisdom determines our choice to take hold of greatness.

How to Strive for Greatness

Key verse: "Whoever wants to become great among you must be your servant, and whoever wants to be first must be your slave—just as the Son of Man did not come to be served, but to serve, and to give his life as a ransom for many" (Matthew 20:26-28 NIV).

Key truths: Many women in ministry want to be "great" without paying the price that Kingdom greatness demands. The price tag reads "Discipleship: 100%." While I totally understand the desire to avoid painful sacrifice, the reality is, greatness is born out of sacrificial service.

I will never forget the first time I flew first-class. Dan and I were on our way from Florida to North Carolina for a few days of vacation, exhausted, having just returned from a grueling mission trip to Peru. I couldn't wait to get on that plane, grab a pillow, and sleep my way to North Carolina.

The check-in line at our gate was abnormally long. My attitude plummeted until I noticed a man who seemed to be waving at us. "Please step forward," he called, motioning for us to approach the counter. Dan then recognized him as a new member of the church and remembered he was a ticket agent for the airline we were flying. "Where are you headed?" our new best friend asked. When we told him, he promptly moved us from coach to first class and escorted us past all of the other waiting, and now glaring, passengers. Any hesitation on my part quickly faded as he showed us to our seats and instructed the stewardess to take good care of his "pastors." I loved that man!

I soon discovered I was a real person in first-class, assigned to a spacious and extremely comfortable leather recliner where I actually had room to move and breathe without assaulting the person next to me. My meal was not wrapped in paper, and they actually trusted me with real eating utensils. I was presented with cloth napkins, hot food, good movies, current magazines, and a stewardess who seemed totally committed to my comfort. By the end of the flight, I was convinced I was born to fly first-class!

So are you! We were created to live life at its best, to experience true success and greatness as servants of God. Jesus said, "My purpose is to give life in all its fullness" (John 10:10). We cannot begin to understand all God's "fullness" holds, but I do know what He wants for me far exceeds anything I could possibly imagine. And I can imagine a lot!

No matter how or where you serve Him, God is calling you to be His disciple. He is asking for 100-percent commitment—and in return, He will fill your life, now and eternally, with the fullness that comes only through knowing and serving the Master. Don't settle for anything less than all He has for you as you seek Him and strive for greatness.

Application steps:

- Revisit the time when God first called you to ministry. What was your initial reaction and response? If you could choose one word to describe your journey—so far—what would it be? Explain.

- Explain the statement "God is my source." What does that really mean in your life and ministry? What other "sources" have you counted on? Did they lead to success or failure in ministry?

- What "wants" have been a hindrance to your ministry? What steps of obedience have you taken to control those "wants"?

- How would you evaluate the impact of the ministry God has given you?

Memory verse: "A greedy person causes trouble, but the one who trusts the LORD will succeed" (Proverbs 28:25 NCV).

Reflection point: *Spiritual greatness begins in a personal relationship with God that is lived out in service to God. What we are is His gift to us, but how we serve Him, is our gift to Him.*

Record any thoughts or fresh insights concerning the above statement:

_____

_____

_____

Power verses:

Praise him for his acts of power; praise him for his surpassing greatness (Psalm 150:2 NIV).

Listen carefully to wisdom; set your mind on understanding. Cry out for wisdom, and beg for understanding. Search for it like silver, and hunt for it like hidden treasure. Then you will understand respect for the LORD, and you will find that you know God (Proverbs 2:2-5 NCV).

You have allowed me to suffer much hardship, but you will restore me to life again and lift me up from the depths of the earth. You will restore me to even greater honor and comfort me once again (Psalm 71:20-21).

One new truth:

_____

_____

G	God
R	Redeems
E	Eternity
A	Agrees
T	Truth
N	Now
E	Embraced
S	Seeking
S	Success

Adrift
A Life Story by Carmen Meeks

Carmen Meeks *has served in pastoral ministry alongside her husband, Mike Meeks, for the past 25 years. She is currently active in women's ministries at EastLake Community Church in Chula Vista, California, and is making plans to go back to school this fall. Carmen and Mike have two grown children and two grandchildren. Her favorite hobbies are hiking and scrapbooking.*

When I was a little girl, my family spent many summer days exploring hiking trails in the mountains of the Pacific Northwest. Our dessert at the end of the trail was often a swim in an icy-fresh mountain lake. We'd whoop with shock and joy as we dipped our sweaty bodies into the clear, cold waters fed by nearby snowfields. After cooling down, we'd spend the afternoon hunting for salamanders and tadpoles or engineering a raft from floating logs. We'd launch our logs Huck Finn style, by pushing away from shore with a strong tree branch. Once our pole could no longer reach bottom, we were adrift, dependent on a stiff mountain breeze or another cold swim to get us back to shore.

I've felt adrift lately. Like I've been pushed away from the familiar comfort of the shoreline into deep water with no sail, no rudder, no power, and no paddle. It seems as if I am floating in deep, dark water, waiting for a breeze to push me in a new direction.

I lost my moorings when our kids left home. My husband is lead pastor of a growing church in Chula Vista, California. We've been here eight years, transplants from the Northwest. Two years ago, our daughter married a great guy she met while attending San Diego State University, and they settled in his hometown of Boca Raton, Florida. (In my opinion, it should be illegal for East Coast guys to infiltrate West Coast schools and steal away our daughters.) Then last year, our son, who had been serving as Creative Arts Director on our church staff, moved his family back to the Northwest, where we raised him. He is planting a new church there and had the gall to take his wife and our two grandkids with him! My nest was suddenly and completely empty, and I didn't feel like taking flight. Instead, I felt grounded, saddened, and very alone.

Now, don't get me wrong. I am blessed in many ways. I have a loving husband and wonderful adult children who have each chosen fabulous spouses. Best of all, I have two adorable grandkids. My gripe is that it now involves a plane ride in order for me to hug and kiss any of them. Although I am surrounded by a loving and supportive church family, I miss my kids, their spouses, and my grandkids every single day.

You might think that as a pastor's wife I would have plenty of responsibilities to keep me busy and distracted from self-pity. You would be right. I can serve my church family in many ways. In fact, I think I've served for some amount of time in just about every department of our church—except men's ministries. Heck, I even contributed to that area by ministering to my man from home!

Two years ago, after serving on our church staff for a number of years, I decided to turn my job over to another competent woman and return to a volunteer role in the church. I am now free to travel with my husband, and the stress level at home is much lower since we are not always running in opposite directions.

But I've been drifting, floating, waiting for a fresh wind to fill my sail and take me into my next port of call.

Over the years, I've learned that it pays to wait for God's guidance. My husband and I often remind ourselves that if we haven't received new directions from the Lord, we are to remain faithful to the last assignment we received from Him. This past year I've continued to lead a woman's group, serve on our prayer team, and teach two-year-olds. I was even able to go on my first international missions trip, a home-building trip for tsunami victims in Thailand. I've been active but restless, sensing the need for a renewed vision of who I am and what God has called me to in this new season of my life. Would I stay in my safe, familiar surroundings or choose a brand new trail into unfamiliar territory?

Three people strongly influenced my thinking. Last New Year's Eve, my daughter said, "Mom, this is a time for you to discover who you are as a woman of God, apart from being a wife and mom." John Eldredge's book *Waking the Dead* showed me God is glorified when we are living from the heart, being fully alive and true to who God created us to be, not what we think others expect us to be. Dr. Judah Folkman ignored criticism from his fellow researchers, investing 20 years of his life in the unique idea that cancerous tumors generate new blood vessels in order to grow. His recent breakthroughs in the treatment of cancer have now put him in the forefront of the fight for a cure. His encouragement: "The key is to choose a problem that is worth persistent effort." My prayer became, *Lord, I want to be the woman you have created me to be, free from the expectations of others, living from the heart, investing my life wisely for Your glory.*

God reveals Himself to us in unexpected moments. My epiphany occurred while sitting on the floor of the Atlanta airport, reading *The Bookseller of Kabul* by Asne Seirstad. My building trip to Thailand had taken me into a Muslim village, where my interest in the lifestyle of Muslim women led me to pick up Seirstad's bestseller. As I sat on the hard floor, surrounded by other weary travelers in various positions of discomfort, I read that three-quarters of the population of Afghanistan can neither read nor write. At that moment, I felt something resonate deep in my heart. I suddenly found myself weeping as my heart opened up to the knowledge that ever since I was a little girl, I have wanted to be a teacher. I set my dream aside while my husband

and I planted a church in Kirkland, Washington, while we raised our children, while I worked to help put my husband through seminary, and while we re-established our lives and ministry in Southern California. I now felt God inviting me to fulfill the dream He had placed in my heart many years ago.

I'm going back to school this fall. I'm going to be a teacher. It feels so natural, so comfortable, and so right. It combines my love for learning, for God's Word, for children, for the people of the world. It is part of who I am in addition to being a wife and a mom. It is something that has always been in my heart. It is my next right step. I am excited to set my sail to this fresh wind and see where this new adventure leads.

🕊 🕊 🕊

Endure the Storms

I really hate storms—of any kind! Tornadoes were a common occurrence in the small Texas town where I grew up. Years later, after moving to South Florida, I experienced storms like none other—hurricanes with winds that could level an entire community in one sweep. Over the years, my life storms have been the source of great pain, often leaving broken relationships, shattered dreams, and emotional debris in their wake. I've always hoped "this storm" would be the last. It never has been.

Ministry is filled with storms of one kind or another and is rarely boring. Ministry must occasionally be messy and tumultuous, or it is not real ministry. In his letter to the church at Corinth, Paul describes the types of storms we can expect to endure, not only as believers but as servants of God in ministry:

> In everything we do we try to show that we are true ministers of God. We patiently endure troubles and hardships and calamities of every kind. We have been

beaten, been put in jail, faced angry mobs, worked to exhaustion, endured sleepless nights, and gone without food. We have proved ourselves by our purity, our understanding, our patience, our kindness, our sincere love, and the power of the Holy Spirit. We have faithfully preached the truth. God's power has been working in us. We have righteousness as our weapon, both to attack and to defend ourselves. We serve God whether people honor us or despise us, whether they slander us or praise us. We are honest, but they call us impostors. We are well known, but we are treated as unknown. We live close to death, but here we are, still alive. We have been beaten within an inch of our lives. Our hearts ache, but we always have joy. We are poor, but we give spiritual riches to others. We own nothing, and yet we have everything (2 Corinthians 6:4-10).

As women in ministry, we sometimes respond halfheartedly to the call of God, refusing to relinquish our hidden agenda that's riddled with self-promoting conditions. We allow these narcissistic stipulations to traipse in and out of our heart desires and thought processes, putting wrong attitudes and impure motives into life and ministry. We desperately try to avoid rocking the boat, we elude sacrificial service, we evade every storm possible, and we even question where God is in the midst of the storm.

When a storm hits, we respond as if God has somehow been caught off guard. The storm makes no sense. We can't explain why terminal illness strikes godly people. We don't understand how our strongest friends can suddenly become our loudest critics. The anguish of a broken marriage or the overwhelming heartbreak of a prodigal child drives us to doubt God's purpose, plan, and provision amid the storms of a life poured out in ministry. Let's face it—when it comes to faith and riding the waves of the storm, we are surely weaklings. But we are certainly not without hope!

The Bible is filled with men and women who were storm survivors—true ministers of God who endured great pain and weathered intense life storms because they chose to follow Him. The apostle Paul is a prime example of someone well acquainted with the ins and outs of enduring storms. Before he met Jesus Christ on the road to Damascus, Paul persecuted and murdered Christians. Then God interrupted his life, changing him from a rabid enemy of Christianity and persecutor of Christians into a radically obedient servant and full-time minister. Everything changed in Paul's life as he was given a new vision filled with purpose, power...and storms.

Like Paul, we may sometimes feel as if we are being torn to pieces under the pressure of circumstances. However, his challenge to the Romans compels us to re-examine our perspective and response to the storms that come our way:

> We can rejoice, too, when we run into problems and trials, for we know that they are good for us—they help us learn to endure. And endurance develops strength of character in us, and character strengthens our confident expectation of salvation (Romans 5:3-4).

Notice Paul indicates we can "learn" to endure. Endurance is neither an inherited trait nor a quality without cost. Endurance has a hefty price tag.

Because grain was a key food source to the Romans, threshing grain was a natural part of every day in ancient Rome. In ancient depictions of this activity, one man is always seen stirring up the sheaves while another rides over them in a crude cart equipped with rollers instead of wheels. Sharp stones and rough bits of iron were attached to these wheels to separate the husks from the grain. This simple cart was called a "tribulum." This is the word from which we get the word "tribulation."

No Roman ever used his tribulum as a tool of destruction—only refinement! The same is true of God. He uses our trials and storms as tools of refinement to build in us a holy endurance beyond any human staying power. The word "endure" comes from two Greek words that, when combined, give the meaning "to remain under."

> God calls us to a heavenly perspective on the tough times in life. He calls us to see them as He sees them—opportunities for Him to be illustrated in human terms.

Endurance is the capacity to stay under the load, to remain in the circumstances without running away or looking for the easy way out. Ministry demands an endurance that can come only from being in the trenches with those to whom we minister.

Endurance is never passive. It is the picture of a soldier staying in the heat of the battle under terrible opposition but still pressing forward to gain the victory! When life is hard, we tend to adopt an escapist attitude. I have to admit that when a storm hits, my first question tends to be, "Where is the nearest exit?" Paul is encouraging us to endure, to stand firm and be steadfast as the storm does God's work in us.

Storms touch every life. Bad things really do happen to both godly and ungodly people. It sometimes seems unjust that unbelievers seem to prosper, sailing through life on serene waters of beauty when those who faithfully serve God are battered and beaten by storms. While it is a reality that life storms slam our faith against the shores of doubt and fear, it is just as true that those storms offer fresh strength to those who embrace the waves of pain and remain faithful in the fierce winds of turmoil. Every crisis—every storm—is an opportunity to trust God. In fact, God calls us to a heavenly perspective on the tough times in life. He calls us to see them as He sees them—opportunities for Him to be illustrated in human terms. How can we harness and use the hard moments? How can we trust God's heart when we cannot see His hand? What choices must we make in order to extract endurance from the storms of life?

First Choice: Count on Storms to Come

As women in ministry, we must recognize and accept the truth that storms are a natural part of our calling. The apostle Paul writes,

> In everything we do we try to show that we are true ministers of God. We patiently endure troubles and hardships and calamities of every kind. We have been beaten, been put in jail, faced angry mobs, worked to exhaustion, endured sleepless nights, and gone without food (2 Corinthians 6:4-5).

We sometimes buy the lie that freedom from trials is payment due or wages earned in return for obedience and faithfulness in ministry. The trials of life—the dark times—offer the opportunity to make eternal investments that will produce eternal returns! In other words, God entrusts each earthly crisis to us for our eternal good. He allows and uses the bad things in life to chip away everything that is not part of our eternal character.

Faith that is tested and frequently exercised is a strong faith. Part of our faith training is on the waves of vicious storms. "Do not be surprised at the painful things you are now suffering. These things are testing your faith" (1 Peter 4:12-13 ICB). God is not committed to our comfort but rather to the forging of His character in us through fiery tests. Paul was tested many times, resulting in his great wisdom and strength as a follower of God. In fact, in his writings, he gives detailed accountings of the trials we can expect to face.

Some Trials Come as Part of Daily Life

Paul calls them "troubles," or more literally translated, "sheer physical pressure." He warns that there will be "hardships, sorrows and calamities of every kind" and that we may find ourselves in "a too narrow place." The picture here is of an army caught in a narrow and rocky passageway with no room to maneuver. We feel there is no way of escape from the walls of life closing in, crushing us under their weight.

Storms come in all shapes and sizes. The lab report comes back malignant. The school calls, demanding you pick up your child, who has just been expelled. Your husband informs you he no longer wants to be married to you. The church advises you it is time to move on. Financial disaster seems certain, while dependable friends seem to vanish. Still—He is enough.

Yes, trials can be suffocating. However, huge problems are sometimes just a series of small problems struggling to get out. I have decided that a day without a crisis is a total loss. Daily life is full of tiny irritations—little pieces of heavenly sandpaper designed to rub us, refining and defining who we really are. We need to embrace those sandpaper moments and sift through them for the treasures they hold. They are for our good!

Some Trials Come as Part of Our Faith

Admittedly, many of us in North America know little about suffering for the sake of our faith in God. However, there are many who do, living each day with the possibility of persecution, knowing it may be their last one on earth. In 2 Corinthians 6:5, Paul vividly describes the cost of serving God. "We have been beaten, been put in jail, faced angry mobs, worked to exhaustion…" Paul is describing trials that many of us know little about—trials that come because of our faith in Jesus Christ.

I witnessed this kind of trial in Mexico, where it is common for Christians to be imprisoned, persecuted, and even killed because of their faith. My husband and I were invited to teach a conference for pastors and their wives in Chiapas, Mexico. On the first day of the conference, we met a pastor who was beside himself with excitement because he had persuaded several men from his village to attend the conference with him the next day. For months, he had prayed and encouraged these fellow pastors to attend the training conference. This precious servant was rejoicing in the fact that God had heard and answered his prayers.

When Dan and I arrived the next morning, the first person we saw was this same man kneeling in the dirt, weeping and wailing, crying out to God. We knelt beside him and wrapped our arms around him as he poured out his pain. One of the pastors had been killed the night before because of his plans to attend the conference. As we began to offer words of comfort at the loss of his friend, this precious man of God slowly raised his tear-stained face to ours. "You don't understand. I am not weeping because of my friend's death. He was allowed to give his life—a precious sacrifice of obedient service—and is today in heaven with Jesus Christ. I am weeping because the other men heard of his death and now refuse to attend the conference. They are afraid. How can we reach the people of Mexico with such weak faith?" The extraordinary faith of this man had been forged in the fires of pain, loss, and suffering. The storms of persecution had left him strong and faithful, willing to surrender his very life in service and endure whatever it took to bring men and women to God.

Some Trials Come Because of Our Sin

Paul states,

> We have proved ourselves by our purity, our understanding, our patience, our kindness, our sincere love, and the power of the Holy Spirit. We have faithfully preached the truth. God's power has been working in us. We have righteousness as our weapon, both to attack and to defend ourselves (2 Corinthians 6:6-7).

When we allow sin and disobedience to dwell in our hearts and minds, we invite trials and darkness to take up residence in our lives. Cherished sin cultivates powerless ministry, while spiritual integrity gives spiritual power. Righteousness—living in the power of the Holy Spirit—provides a hedge of protection against the darkness. We must keep short books on sin in order to access the strength that will see us through the storms of life and ministry.

Storms will come, and bad things will happen. Where is God? God is where He has always been and always will be—in the midst of every storm, our Savior and Redeemer hiding us in the shelter of His arms. As a woman in ministry, you are certainly no stranger to pain. It doesn't matter if you minister to one or one thousand. You may be on the staff of a large church or responsible for unlocking the doors of your small country church. Ministry is measured by your obedience to God's call in your life, not your response to the call of man or the evaluation of humanity. The battle, while long and hard, belongs to God. Rest in Him and let His strength sustain you.

Second Choice: Count on Strength for the Storms

Our "storm expert," Paul, in his writings to the church at Corinth, offers six conditions that, when met, will enable us to endure the storms of life and ministry.

Live a Pure Life

> We have proved ourselves by our purity... (2 Corinthians 6:6).

Notice that purity is the first condition Paul lists. He is sending a clear message. Integrity in ministry is the result of a heart that is wholly committed to purity. A clean heart unleashes the authority of God within us and causes His power to surge through us. Impurity always corrodes stability, while purity generates a supernatural strength. It is that power and stability that keeps us from falling.

The prayer of our hearts should be, "Create in me a pure heart, O God, and renew a steadfast spirit within me" (Psalm 51:10 NASB). Notice the psalmist links a pure heart with a steadfast spirit. The correlation is unmistakable. "Steadfast" means "fixed or unchanging" and defines the kind of strength that can only be found in a right relationship with God. Stability is essential when the blustery winds of life storms are raging. While some trials are the result of our sin, other storms come to uncover that cherished sin we try so hard to bury. Either way, the purpose of the storm is always to purify—then empower! If we refuse to deal with the sin in our lives, God will *urge* us toward obedience by allowing the storms to come.

Seek Understanding

> We have proved ourselves by...our understanding...
> (2 Corinthians 6:6).

Understanding is only as good as its place of origin. Human understanding is limited and tainted. Godly understanding is infinite and unspoiled. Our greatest lessons are learned in the midst of the greatest storms. I know you have heard that statement many times—but is it a living reality in your life? A teacher was asked a question by one of his students, who had come across Deuteronomy 6:6: "These commandments that I give you today are to be upon your hearts" (NIV). The student asked, "Why does it say to put God's commandments *upon* our hearts instead of *in* our hearts?" The wise teacher responded, "It is not within man's power to deposit truth directly into his heart. All we can do is place truth on the surface of the heart so that when the heart breaks, it will fall in."

Every circumstance that results in brokenness is designed to produce clearer truth, greater self-control and fresh understanding. When it comes to powerful ministry, God uses the most broken servants to accomplish His greatest work. We can face every storm with confidence, knowing that God will redeem it for understanding and truth!

Learn to Be Patient

> We have proved ourselves by...our patience...(2 Corinthians 6:6).

I must confess I am not the epitome of patience! In fact, I hate to wait on anyone or anything, which undoubtedly explains the presence of certain storms and trials in my life. James had the same problem but a much better attitude!

> Consider it pure joy, my brothers, whenever you face trials of many kinds, because you know that the testing of your faith develops perseverance. Perseverance must finish its work so that you may be mature and complete, not lacking anything (James 1:2-3 NIV).

I tend to consider it pure joy when I can *escape* trials of many kinds! However, James tells us that trials can and should be faced with patience and an attitude of joy. Not joy *for* the trials, but joy *in* the trials! Don't miss this vital truth. Joy is a chosen attitude that recognizes the powerful truth that trials are not punishment but opportunities for growth.

Trials are a test, a measurement of growth, and a producer of patience. Patience gives God permission to work and expects to be tested. We go to great lengths to avoid trials, to shelter ourselves from the storms of life. As a result, we are spiritually immature. God will not build our character without our cooperation, nor will He work in us without our permission! We must surrender! We must invite Him to work—and then by faith, patiently embrace that work in our lives. Warren Wiersbe writes, "When God permits his children to go through the furnace, He keeps his eye on the clock and His hand on the thermostat!"

Doubt puts our circumstances between us and God, while faith puts God between us and our circumstances. I asked one of the great prayer warriors in my life what she does when doubt knocks at the door of her life. She smiled and said, "I just ask Jesus to get the door for me." Patience comes when we give up the responsibility for the outcome to God!

Practice Kindness

In the midst of a storm, our desperate hearts cry out for someone to care. More people come to Christ during a crisis than at any other time in life. The most powerful ministry is found in the midst of the greatest pain, which means that we need to view each crisis as an opportunity for God to work through our kindness.

Kindness is simply compassion at work, love in action. As women in ministry, we need to constantly refocus our success-targeted eyes, crucify each arrogant heart motive, and pray for awareness of the needs around us. The choice to minister that is, in any way, made on the basis of self-promotion, is worth nothing and becomes offensive to God. I often wonder just how amazed we will be when we get to heaven and find the unlikely, unknown, but wholly devoted servants of God exalted above all others—rewarded for their quiet and often unseen acts of kindness.

A certain preacher described his mother as a woman of great kindness and compassion. One day, he recounted, he came home from school to find her sitting at the kitchen table with an elderly, homeless man. Apparently, she had gone shopping, met the man on the way, and invited him home for a warm meal. During their conversation the visitor said, "I wish there were more people in the world like you." The woman said quickly, "Oh, there are! You just have to look for them!" The old man simply shook his head and smiled. "But lady, I didn't look for you. You looked for me!"

Needs constantly parade before us day after day, but we don't notice them! We are so busy serving God that we fail to see the broken lambs He sends our way. We view them as intrusions, annoying interruptions in our very important ministry schedule. These uninvited and unscheduled guests may very well be divine appointments sent by God and our greatest opportunity to serve Him. The warning of Hebrews 13:2 is a haunting one: "Remember to welcome strangers, because some who have done this have welcomed angels without knowing it" (NCV). I wonder just how many angels we have missed because we are too busy!

Perhaps we fail to be kind because we simply do not care enough. Jesus says if we really love God, we will really love each other. Kindness and compassion are directly related to the health of our personal relationship with Jesus Christ. The truths in 1 John 4:20 are clear:

> If someone says, "I love God," and hates his brother, he is a liar; for he who does not love his brother whom he has seen, how can he love God whom he has not seen?

The last part of that verse can be translated "for he who does not love his brother whom he has seen, *cannot* love God whom he has not seen." We cannot love God without loving others. When we love others, we love God. We can be very religious and still not care enough!

Kindness does not look for reasons. Compassion doesn't ask for limitations. It searches for opportunities to work. The people in your world do not need condemnation. They need compassion! The people in your world do not need a sermon in words—but a sermon lived out and often silently preached through acts of kindness.

Experience and Practice Love

> Always be humble, gentle, and patient, accepting each other in love. You are joined together with peace through the Spirit, so make every effort to continue together in this way (Ephesians 4:2-3 NCV).

We need not only God in the midst of the storm, we need each other! The essence of true love is tested within the context of relationships. How we handle relationships exhibits the depth and validity of God's love at work in and through us. As women in ministry, someone will always be disappointed, disgruntled, or displeased with what we do or how we do it. We have a choice to make. We can either honor God by waging peace or venerate Satan by entertaining conflict in relationships. God is committed to unity. If we don't make "every effort" to eradicate discord, a storm may come to help us do so.

I have a friend who raises and works with horses. She once explained how a group of thoroughbred horses confronts an enemy. They stand in a circle, noses together, and with their hind legs, they kick out at the enemy. Donkeys do just the opposite—they face the enemy and kick each other! Enough said.

Count on God's Power

> LORD, even when I have trouble all around me, you will keep me alive. When my enemies are angry, you will reach down and save me by your power (Psalm 138:7 NCV).

As women in ministry, we must be careful to recognize and remember the source of power that fuels ministry. It is not found in our talent, ability, position, or title. Our only source of true power for life is found in the person of God through the control of the

Holy Spirit. "Power" literally means "strength and authority." When we depend upon and minister from the strength and authority of God—instead of our own—we will stand strong when the storm hits. One of the Holy Spirit's most important jobs is to comfort and sustain us in every situation—if we allow Him to do so. I do fairly well when the skies are clear and the seas are calm. However, when the waves hit, I can forget every promise I know, doubt every truth I've ever learned, and quickly lose my sense of direction.

While swimming in the ocean one time, my father-in-law was caught in a school of jellyfish and stung many times. Panicked and confused, he dove underwater and began swimming furiously, but he soon lost his sense of direction. Time was running out when Dad realized there was only one way to survive. Forcing himself to relax, he began to float. It was only seconds until the dark water grew lighter. By swimming toward that light, Dad made it to the surface and safety, just before passing out.

Have you ever felt that way in ministry—caught in an excruciating situation, stung by harsh criticism and painful betrayal? Panic sets in, and paralyzing confusion strips your heart bare. You swim furiously toward unrealistic expectations and unrealized dreams, but nothing changes. There is no vision, no power, and no passion. Lost and confused, you are forced to do the very thing you should have done first—relax and rest in Him. When the strong waves hit, when we lose our way in the midst of a storm, we must stop, look for the Light, and swim toward Him!

> The best way to *get ready* for a storm is to *stay ready* for a storm. And the best preparation for tomorrow's storm is to plug the truth of God into our lives today!

In Scripture, God's truth is often described as a "lamp" or "light." The reason is clear. "Truth" literally means "integrity or deeply rooted righteousness." "Righteousness" simply means "right living." The presence of God's truth dispels spiritual darkness and unleashes the power of God to work, producing His righteousness and integrity in us. Simply put, if we want to experience God's power, we must know and obey God's truth. It is a mighty weapon in weathering storms. "We have faithfully preached the truth. God's power has been working in us. We have righteousness as our weapon, both to attack and to defend ourselves" (2 Corinthians 6:7).

Truth roots itself deeply, providing not only stability and direction, but every weapon needed for spiritual warfare. Without His truth active and alive in our lives, we are defenseless and powerless against the ruthless attacks of the enemy. When we step into ministry, we are stepping into enemy territory.

I am told that the Holy Land is extremely dry. Water is precious and hard to find, and trees growing there are amazingly strong because their roots must reach deep into the earth in order to find a water source. In southern Florida, however, where we lived for many years, water is everywhere. When Hurricane Andrew hit Ft. Lauderdale, we lost several large palm trees. They looked strong, but their roots were shallow, and as a result, they were easily toppled by the storm. Ministry is much the same! To withstand the storms of ministry, we must be committed to deepening our roots in God by allowing His truth to grow freely in our lives.

When hurricane warnings are issued, the grocery stores immediately fill with frantic customers in search of bread, water, and canned goods. Batteries and plywood fly off of hardware store shelves. Lines at the ATM machines and gas pumps block traffic and fan tempers. Panic sets in and reason is lost. Why? People are not prepared for the storm.

Don't wait! You never know when the next storm will hit. The best way to *get ready* for a storm is to *stay ready* for a storm. And the best preparation for tomorrow's storm is to plug the truth of God into our lives today!

Third Choice: Count on Joy in the Storms!

When golf balls were first manufactured, their covers were smooth. Golfers soon discovered that after a ball had been roughed up a bit, they were able to get more distance out of it. Manufacturers then began producing golf balls with dimpled covers. Life and ministry are a lot like that. It takes some rough spots to make us go our farthest. It takes some storms to teach us God is faithful and will provide the strength to stand firm.

The apostle Paul was despised, slandered, mistreated, abused, and poor. He had every right to be angry and distressed, but instead he chose joy: "We own nothing, and yet we have everything" (2 Corinthians 6:10).

I never fully understood the amazing truth behind Paul's words because I had never really lived their truth—until 1995, when I found myself sitting at the bottom of a deep, dark pit. Clinical depression, the psychologists and physicians called it. The name was irrelevant to me. All I knew was that it was the most hellish place I had ever been and I had absolutely no idea how to escape. I was paralyzed and totally helpless—the perfect setting for a miracle! Sitting at the feet of Jesus, stripped of my human efforts and impotent plans, I discovered the life-changing truth that He did not come to eliminate the storms in my life. He came to fill those storms with His presence. I was not delivered *from* that pit until I was first delivered *in* that pit.

The highest joy will come through the greatest pain. The greater the pain, the more we are forced to search for and cling to the hand of God! That only happens when we choose the right attitude toward pain. Here it is!

> Whenever trouble comes your way, let it be an opportunity for joy. For when your faith is tested, your endurance has a chance to grow (James 1:2-3).

When was the last time you threw a party to celebrate the trials and storms in ministry? Hurricane parties are common practice in southern Florida. Knowing that the loss of electricity was likely, we would empty our refrigerator, inviting neighbors and friends to join us in celebrating the fact that the storm had come and gone and we were still standing. God's ways are higher than our ways, and most human reactions are in direct opposition to the paradoxical ways of

God. Honestly, there are times when what He has asked me to do simply does not make sense—to me. And there we find the problem. Faith is a matter of blind obedience, not human logic.

At the heart of every storm is victory—just waiting to be claimed! The words of James offer the perfect perspective for every life storm. As I mentioned in an earlier chapter, I can't sew a straight seam, so when my sister began doing needlepoint, I was duly impressed. During a recent visit she pulled out her latest project, a small Christmas pillow. It was beautiful! "Turn it over," she said. The back was a mess of knots and mismatched thread going in every direction. Then the thought hit me. We question God, asking why life is such a mess, railing against every emotional "knot" and questioning the circumstances that don't seem to match our lives. I can almost hear Him say, "Yes, but you should see it from my point of view. It is beautiful!"

As women in ministry and daughters of the King, we have a different point of view for every life experience. It is a manger, a cruel cross, an empty tomb, and eternity itself. That viewpoint changes everything. It makes our hearts sing and our souls dance with the truth that we can always count on His joy in us to face the storms around us! It is the reason we do what we do.

What storm is raging in your life? What step do you need to take in order to exchange your strength for His? Your Father stands ready to meet you in your darkest hour. He longs to wrap His arms around you until the winds die down and the waves are stilled. Surrender. Yield to His presence and power. Celebrate the storm that is dashing your battered life on the shores of His unyielding love—and praise Him. He really does provide the strength and power to endure every storm.

How to Endure the Storms

Key verse: "God is our refuge and strength, a very present help in trouble" (Psalm 46:1 NRSV).

Key truths: The only survivor of a shipwreck was washed up on a small, uninhabited island. He feverishly prayed for God's rescue, but with every day that passed, his hope weakened. Exhausted, he eventually managed to build a little hut out of driftwood to protect himself from the elements and to store his few possessions. One day, after scavenging for food, he arrived home to find his little hut in flames, the smoke rolling up to the sky. Everything was lost. Stunned with grief and anger, the man cried, "God, how could you do this to me!" The next morning, he woke to the sound of a ship approaching the island. It had come to rescue him. "How did you know I was here?" the weary man asked. "We saw your smoke signal," they replied.

Storms are for our good. We will either become storm survivors or storm statistics. The choice really is ours to make. We can stop telling God how big our storm is and start telling the storm just how big our God is. The key to enduring storms is to embrace each one that comes, knowing it contains a seed of victory and can yield triumph.

I know you have repeatedly heard and have probably even taught the truth that we are strengthened by our storms. Honestly, there have been times when I felt as if I would explode if one more person told me to praise God for my storm. Looking back, however, there is absolutely no doubt that my greatest growth has come during my worst life storms. Each storm has become a spiritual marker, a testament to the sufficiency and faithfulness of God. It is from those markers that a powerful ministry is shaped.

Application steps:

- As a woman in ministry, describe your greatest life storm. What was your response to that storm? What truth did the storm yield?

- Examine the following list of character traits. How have your life storms encouraged growth in each area? Explain.

Purity _____

Love _____

Power _____

Patience _____

Kindness _____

Understanding _____

Memory verse: "God is our refuge and strength, a very present help in trouble" (Psalm 46:1 NRSV).

Reflection point: *Endurance is never passive. It is the picture of a soldier staying in the heat of the battle under terrible opposition but still pressing forward to gain the victory!*

Record any thoughts or fresh insights concerning the above statement:

_____

_____

Power verses:

When the storm has swept by, the wicked are gone, but the righteous stand firm forever (Proverbs 10:25 NIV).

You have been a defense for the helpless, a defense for the needy in his distress, a refuge from the storm, a shade from the heat… (Isaiah 25:4 NASB).

Be merciful to me, O God, be merciful to me, for in you my soul takes refuge; in the shadow of your wings I will take refuge, until the destroying storms pass by (Psalm 57:1 NRSV).

One new truth:

_____

_____

S   Surrender
T   Totally
O   Obey
R   Radically
M   Magnificent
S   Strength

Consider It Joy
A Life Story by Micca Campbell

Micca Campbell *is a wife, mother, and a national speaker with Proverbs 31 Ministries. Her passion is to know God and be one with Him while leading others into that same kind of relationship, until all are free in Christ. For more information about Micca, visit the speaker section at www. proverbs31.org.*

Consider it pure joy, my brothers, whenever you face trials of many kinds, because you know that the testing of your faith develops perseverance. Perseverance must finish its work so that you may be mature and complete, not lacking anything (James 1:2-4 NIV).

Whether a test from God, a result of my own sin, or because I live in a fallen world, the storms in my life have taught me how helpless I am and how much I need Him. Once we experience His comfort, we are then able to comfort others in the same way, with the same heart, and the same character of Christ. Many of the storms earlier in my life produced a lot of "little deaths." At the time, I didn't see their significance—but looking back, I now realize that all of those little deaths were preparing me for the biggest death of all…the loss of my husband.

I met Porter through a friend from work, Amanda, a newlywed who owned only one car. She offered to buy my gas if I could bring her home each afternoon. I agreed. One day, Amanda invited me in to meet her husband. I met not only her husband but one of his friends, Porter. The first thing I noticed about Porter was his picture-perfect smile. He was so good-looking. Instantly, I knew I wanted a date, so Amanda made the arrangements. The next day at work, I couldn't wait to hear if Porter wanted to go out with me as well. He did! I was so excited I could barely keep my mind on my work the rest of the day.

It was love at first sight. We were married within the year. Even though we were poor as church mice, we were so happy. It felt as if we were the only two people in the world. Nothing could touch us. We lived on love and big dreams, one of which was to have children. That dream became a reality with the birth of a beautiful baby boy. With another mouth to feed, Porter began taking side jobs, one of which was working with my brother-in-law, who needed someone to waterproof the basement of his home. Since Porter worked for a waterproofing company, he was perfect for the job. On his first day, he woke me up to tell me he was leaving and would probably work till dinnertime. He was so cute. I can still see him in my mind's eye, baseball cap on his head with his brown wavy hair curled around it. He bent down and kissed me goodbye. I had no idea it would be our last kiss.

Porter worked all day applying a black, sticky paste to the basement's outer walls. Consequently, his entire body was covered as well. The paste was highly flammable, but he felt sure that the fumes would evaporate since he was working outdoors. My brother-in-law arrived home early from work. Surprised to see that Porter was almost finished, he quickly changed clothes and jumped down in the ditch with him to help him out. With only five feet of wall left to go, tragedy struck.

It was a cool fall day in Tennessee, but by late afternoon it had warmed up quite a bit. Suddenly, the air conditioner clicked on, igniting fumes and causing the ditch to explode. Both my husband and my brother-in-law were badly burned.

At the hospital, the doctor took my sister and me into a counseling room where he delivered his diagnosis. My brother-in-law was not burned as badly as Porter and was expected to recover. On the other hand, Porter's entire body was burned. The doctor couldn't offer much hope and said that even if he lived, he would probably not keep his arms. "How bad are they?" I asked. He didn't mince words. "They are burned down to the bone."

It may have been selfish, but I didn't care if Porter could never hold his son or me again. I just wanted him to live. Day and night I cried out to God, "Please, Lord, let him live!" However, during a skin-graft surgery, Porter went into cardiac arrest, his weakened body unable to take any more traumas. After he lay on life support for eight days in the burn center at Vanderbilt Hospital, I found the strength to allow his life-support machine to be turned off. Sitting beside my husband's bed, I suddenly realized he had gone to be with the Father many days ago. It was time for me to let go.

It seemed so unnatural to be a widow at the age of 21. All my hopes and dreams were now buried inside a casket. It's funny— the newspaper called me a "survivor." I didn't feel like a survivor. It felt more like I was dead too. That's what I wanted—to be dead. Day after day, night after night, I ached for my husband and longed to be with him. I became angry with the God I had loved since I was a child. Shaking my fist in His face, I felt betrayed and abandoned by both my God and my husband.

In time, I realized that God had neither left nor betrayed me. He met me in my pain, lifted my head, and set me on higher ground. I grew stronger and stronger until I came to understand the words of Corrie Ten Boom, who was held prisoner in a Nazi concentration camp. "There is no pit so deep that He is not deeper still." Through the death of my husband, God's constant presence, and my surrendered will, death and suffering was transformed into life and hope, enabling me to become a true survivor of death.

Joy and healing can be found by believing God loves me in all things and is working for my good to conform me to the image of Christ. Instead of asking, "What am I going to do?" I am learning to ask, "What is God going to do?" in the midst of a storm. He is not working to destroy me—but to re-create me, making me strong and Christlike so I'm able to finish the race. I am learning to choose life by trusting Him and not my circumstances. He has a plan, and His plan can be trusted.

"Are you sure?" you ask. Just look at the evidence. I have a wonderful new husband, two beautiful children, an awesome ministry—and a heart that believes my Lord is good...all the time.

A Final Thought:

The Power of Purpose

The story is told of three men who were working on a large building project. One was asked, "What are you doing?" The man answered, "I'm helping put up this great stone wall." The second man offered, "I'm mixing mortar." When the third worker was asked what he was doing, he responded, "I'm building a cathedral to the glory of God." Ministry is greatly influenced by the attitude and perspective of the minister. We can and must learn to choose our inner attitude regardless of outer circumstances. Ministry is worship, an altar upon which we lay our calling from God as an offering of praise to Him.

I love being a woman in ministry! Yes, ministry is filled with hard times, but it is also filled with unspeakable joy. If we are not careful, though, our perspective in ministry will be determined by the pain of ministry. Hurt will overshadow healing. Anger will devour peace. Discontent will suffocate joy and eventually overshadow purpose.

As women in ministry, we have a timeless message of hope that the world desperately longs to hear. Ministry is a sacred calling and a high privilege. What we do really does matter. If that is true—and it is—then women in ministry should be women of joy. Our hearts should be at joyful rest in every circumstance because we know and serve the God of all circumstances, the Lord of every mountain and Shepherd of every valley.

The First Love

But sadly, my prayer list is filled with women in ministry who are ready to walk away from it all because there is no joy, no purpose, and no power. It seems as if they are living under the burden of circumstances instead of seeing God in the midst of those circumstances. The darkness is closing in as they struggle just to stay afloat on the storm-tossed seas of ministry, much less make progress toward any destination. Resentment is a constant companion, and bitterness shadows each step. Why? Because somewhere along the way, they have lost their first love—and consequently, lost the joy of serving God.

> I know your works, your labor, your patience, and that you cannot bear those who are evil. And you have tested those who say they are apostles and are not, and have found them liars; and you have persevered and have patience, and have labored for My name's sake and have not become weary. Nevertheless I have this against you, that you have left your first love (Revelation 2:2-4 NKJV).

What a stunning indictment—that nothing we do in ministry will please God unless that ministry is an overflow of our first love, Jesus Christ. When we are in love with God, our heart attitude converts our ministry perspective into one of praise and gratitude. I am not talking about the power of positive thinking. I'm talking about a real, honest-to-goodness heart and mind transformation of the attitude and perspective that motivates every step we take in ministry. I'm talking about the power of God, active and present in every circumstance.

A Life That Matters

Refuse to accept a pharisaical religion or a bunch of slot-filling, box-checking rituals. Settle for nothing less than the undeniable presence of God at work in your ministry by cultivating and establishing the godly habits that produce a ministry fueled by God's power and ordered by His purpose:

P Perceive your worth
U Unleash your faith
R Relish Godly discipline
P Pursue God's vision
O Opt for peace
S Strive for greatness
E Endure the storms

Habits are strange critters. Just when you think you have them mastered and firmly in place, some bump in the road of life or ministry knocks you flat, and there you are—staring at the same old pile of defeat and failure. Rest assured that your Father knows and stands ready to "lift you out of the pit of despair, out of the mud and the mire." God will "set your feet on solid ground—higher ground—and give you a new song to sing, a hymn of praise to your God" (Psalm 40:1-3, author's paraphrase).

As these seven habits become a reality *in* you, God will accomplish His plan *through* you! "Many will see what he has done and be astounded. They will put their trust in the LORD" (Psalm 40:3). That's powerful ministry, my friend, and it just doesn't get any better!

I am just like you, a woman in ministry who simply wants what God wants for my life and for every life He allows me to touch.

Like you, my heart's desire is to please Him and to serve Him in such a way that hell is plundered and heaven is populated.

Like you, I want my life to matter, to make a difference in the lives of those seeking God and especially in the lives of those who aren't—because to snatch a pagan who still smells like smoke from the very pit of hell is ministry at its best.

Like you, loving the unlovable and reaching the unreachable is the highest calling I can possibly imagine or dream for this unlikely servant living in this fallen world.

Like you, I not only want to experience the abundant life God freely offers, I choose to be a channel through which He pours that abundance into the lives of others.

Like you, I strive to walk in truth and integrity, knowing that when I fail, He can't.

And together, my friend, we celebrate God's call to be wholly devoted to His purpose, experiencing His power in our ministry.

Journey Ministry

...and as with any journey, there are unseen detours, unexpected stops, and surprising turns in the road—and priceless treasures to be found along the way. I want to encourage you and walk with you, knowing God has gone before us to order each step and keep His eye on every storm.

That's right—no matter where the journey leads, God is there. Rest assured He is Lord of every mountain, Shepherd of every valley, Friend of every wounded heart... and He loves you.

Mary

*M*ary **Southerland** is a pastor's wife, the mother of two, an author, and an international speaker. A dynamic communicator, Mary delivers a powerful message that changes lives. She will make you laugh, cry, and walk away thirsting for more. Through warmth, humor, transparency, and solid biblical teaching, she leads women to discover the powerful truth of God's Word and motivates them to apply it in their daily lives. She is also the founder of Journey Ministry, a teaching ministry dedicated to equipping every woman for her unique journey to the heart of God.

Mary is available to speak for conferences,
retreats and women's events:

Web site: www.marysoutherland.com
E-mail: journeyfriends@cs.com
Phone: 704-843-2934

Acknowledgments

God has used so many women in ministry to impact my life—the list is endless. But my mother was the first. Although she never served on a church staff or even taught a Bible study, my mother was, without a doubt, a woman in ministry. After my father died, she held down three jobs to put food on the table. She made sure that my sister, my brother, and I were in church every Sunday—even when she had to work. She loved me when I was unlovable, delighted in my call to ministry, and today still cheers me on from heaven's balcony. Thank you, Mama! I love you!

Thanks to my husband, Dan. I would have quit long ago and missed the most exciting chapters of my journey to the heart of God without your love and support. Thank you for always believing in me and constantly cheering me on. I adore you!

Thanks to my incredible children, Jered and Danna. You are the heart of my ministry and my greatest teachers. You fill my life with joy. I love you, I cherish you, and I am blessed to be your mom.

Thanks to my sister, Betty McKenzie. You are not only my sister, but my friend and a woman in ministry. Every part of my life—from the ordinary to the extraordinary—is important to you. When I am sick, you call to make sure I am taking care of myself. When I am in the midst of a crisis, I know the phone will ring— and there you are…encouraging me…believing in me…ministering to me. I love you!

Thanks to Kay Warren. You are truly a stunning woman of God, one of my favorite people in the world and my friend. I have watched you walk through fiery trials only to emerge more beautiful and stronger than before. Your joy and authenticity lead me and countless other women to faithfully embrace their identity in and calling from God. Your commitment to God's plan—no matter what the cost—has forever impacted my life.

Thanks to Katie Brazelton, Micca Campbell, Tania Haber, Carmen Meeks, Mary Nash, Rachel Olsen, Kelley Searcy, and Gwen Smith for sharing your life stories. You are a blessing to me and to the kingdom of God.

Thanks to Alison Pond. What a special friend you are to me! Thanks for your listening ear, your caring heart, and your fresh perspective on ministry and life in general!

Thanks to Betty Jean Billingsley. You loved me and believed in me—from the moment we first met. Your quiet strength and gracious spirit have constantly encouraged me to pursue God and His truth.

Thanks to Grace Chavis. Your commitment to prayer and holiness is a benchmark in my life. Thank you for your support and friendship over the years.

Thanks to Corabel Morgan. Thank you for adding my name to your daily prayer list—and keeping it there! Knowing that you pray for me, for my family, and for my ministry every day is a precious gift. Only heaven knows all that God has done in my life through your commitment to pray.

Thanks to Rene Gillming, Kelly Robertson, Sharon Distefano, and Sandy Mayer. Serving with you as pastor's wives at Flamingo Road Church was the ride of a lifetime! I love you all!

Thanks to the Journey Ministry Prayer Warriors! You have literally prayed me through the writing of this book. When I lost five weeks of writing time due to a bout with viral meningitis, you prayed. When the words wouldn't come, you prayed. When meeting the deadline seemed impossible, you prayed. I love you and thank God for your presence in my life.

Thanks to the Harvest House staff. You are simply the best! Your belief in me as an author is simply amazing, and being part of the Harvest House family is a dream come true!

Above all, thank You, Father God, for allowing me to serve You as a woman in ministry. Your grace covers my frailty and inadequacy. Your mercy refreshes my soul and Your love shapes the very fabric of the ministry to which You have called me. May You be glorified in every written word!

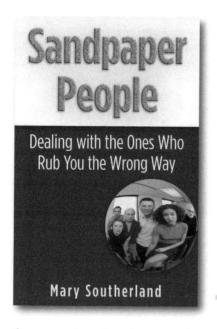

Sandpaper People

*Dealing with
the Ones Who Rub You
the Wrong Way*

Mary Southerland

🙠🙠🙠

*"God, why did You
put these problem people
in my life?"*

The unwanted intrusion of a nosy neighbor…the exasperating call from your least favorite co-worker…the latest mess-up by the relative who doesn't seem to want to change. Talk about rubbing you raw!

If you've run out of ideas for handling your difficult relationships, perhaps it's time to try a fresh approach. Working from a toolbox full of anecdotes and humor, Mary Southerland presents action principles for relating to the abrasive people in your life, such as…

- recognizing their worth
- knowing when to confront
- refusing to walk away

Chapter-by-chapter questions, applications, and journaling suggestions will help you recognize your own sandpaper tendencies and see your sandpaper people for what they are: opportunities from God to grow—while being transformed in the process.

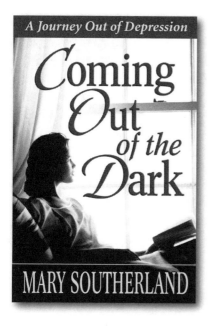

A Journey Out of Depression

Coming Out of the Dark
A Journey Out of Depression
Mary Southerland

🍃🍃🍃

As a pastor's wife and mother of two adorable children, Mary Southerland had a life filled with wonderful things…until clinical depression brought her world crashing down. Mary found herself in a horrible pit, but she also slowly discovered the way out. And now she offers biblical insight and practical steps to freedom with the refreshing transparency of someone who has been there and intimately knows the pain of what you and your family are experiencing.

As one of America's fastest growing health problems, depression touches one in three people. If you struggle with depression, have a loved one dealing with depression, or simply need encouragement during a bleak time of life, *Coming out of the Dark* will help. It will guide you to the One who is light and who will be right beside you to comfort and encourage you from the beginning of your journey to its end—a place of wholeness, joy, and freedom.

More Great Ministry Resources
From Harvest House Publishers

Building an Effective Women's Ministry
Develop a Plan • Gather a Team • Watch God Work

Sharon Jaynes

Do you want to develop or improve a women's ministry but feel overwhelmed by the responsibility? Uncertain about where to start? Sharon Jaynes, vice president of Proverbs 31 Ministries, provides clear answers to nearly any question you can think of and presents the planning tools and confidence-builders you need to succeed. Discover how to identify your ministry's mission; develop a leadership team; avoid burnout and achieve balance; create programs that nurture, reach out, and revive; and much more!

> *"Sharon gives biblically sound, practical ideas*
> *for leading women into a vital and vibrant*
> *relationship with Jesus Christ."*
>
> Tim Clinton,
> president, American Association
> of Christian Counselors
>
> Julie Clinton,
> president, Extraordinary Women

Women Helping Women
A Biblical Guide to Major Issues Women Face

Carol Cornish and Elyse Fitzpatrick

Counsel based on the Scriptures is more powerful than you can imagine. This one-of-a-kind resource helps you share God's comfort, hope, and encouragement from the Bible in response to today's problems—difficult marriages, infertility, divorce, addictions, rebellious teens, care of elderly parents, and many other major life issues. A superb resource for every woman who wants to help, support, and advise other women.

Finding a Mentor, Being a Mentor
Sharing Our Lives as Women of God

Donna Otto

Not only does mentoring help you share the joys and pains of everyday life, it provides a place for you to discuss effective strategies to handle the demands of being a wife, mother, friend, and businesswoman. Bestselling author Donna Otto shows you how to develop and nourish a mentoring relationship that will help you…

- understand God's unique purpose for your life
- make better use of your time, skills, and spiritual gifts
- cultivate a stronger faith and trust in God